THE FLYING MAN
THE GOLDEN AGE OF ISLAM & ITS CONTRIBUTION TO SCIENCE & PHILOSOPHY

Published in the UK by Beacon Books and Media Ltd
Earl Business Centre, Dowry Street, Oldham, OL8 2PF, UK.

Copyright © Akbar Ahmed 2024

The right of Akbar Ahmed to be identified as the author of this work has been asserted in accordance with the Copyright, Designs and Patents Act 1988. All rights reserved. This book may not be reproduced, scanned, transmitted or distributed in any printed or electronic form or by any means without the prior written permission from the copyright owner, except in the case of brief quotations embedded in critical reviews and other non-commercial uses permitted by copyright law.

www.beaconbooks.net

ISBN 978-1-915025-96-8 Paperback
ISBN 978-1-912356-04-1 Hardback
ISBN 978-1-915025-97-5 Ebook

Cataloging-in-Publication record for this book is available from the British Library.

Cover design by Raees Mahmood Khan

Praise for "The Flying Man"

In this inspiring book, Professor Akbar Ahmed continues his personal quest of bridging the gap between the Orient and the West, as he did in his earlier books and projects. Only this time, the author has taken us to the remarkable world of philosophy in which he brings us face-to-face with the great philosophers of the Golden Age and their ideas from differing cultural backgrounds and times.

After reading this excellently written book, it is obvious that we humans, regardless of our backgrounds and affiliations, are similar in our quest for truth, understanding ourselves, and in our "love of wisdom." Professor Akbar has performed an inspiring and noble task in showing this to us in such a fascinating way in a time when differences are being overemphasized and common human values distorted. I really enjoyed reading this wonderful book. Congratulations on this fascinating and timely work.

Dr. Husein ef. Kavazović,
Grand Mufti of the Islamic Community in Bosnia and Herzegovina

Akbar Ahmed powerfully reconstructs Islam's role as the quintessential bridge-builder between the classical and the modern, and between the East and the West. Analyzing the key ideas of several of the greatest Islamic philosophers and their influence on Jewish and Christian thinkers, the book not only challenges stereotypes about Islam but also offers invaluable lessons for today's society—Muslims and non-Muslims alike—on the importance of debate, tolerance, and diversity.

Amitav Acharya, Distinguished Professor of International Relations,
American University, Washington DC

Akbar Ahmed is a Muslim treasure himself. But in this book, he's a treasure hunter excavating the Golden Age of thought and creativity during the Islamic civilization's early period, a period too often ignored by Western scholars.

Sheikh Hamza Yusuf, President and Co-founder of Zaytuna College

Amongst all of his important books, this gem of a book is Ambassador Ahmed's magnum opus, a culmination of his entire bridge-building work and ideas. In accessible language, he introduces us to the masters of antiquity, the champions of Andalucian convivencia and Abrahamic saint-scholars. These are ideal role models for our youth. As a university teacher, I am excited about this important teaching resource. Every library must have this superb book.

Dr. Amineh Hoti Fellow-Commoner, University of Cambridge,
Program Director, Seerat, Higher Education Commission, Pakistan

In a clear and accessible style, Dr. Akbar Ahmed presents a sweeping survey of Islamic thought in what in Western scholarship is called the Golden Age of Islam, dealing not only with some of the most famous Islamic philosophers and Sufis of that Age but also with St. Thomas Aquinas and Maimonides and referring to many later Western figures. He provides a vivid and instructive guide for both Western and Muslim readers to a very fecund and creative period of the Islamic philosophical tradition that has survived to this day.

Professor Seyyed Hossein Nasr,
George Washington University, Washington, DC

How can we grow to humanize our science? How can we solve the paradox of our time? The cyberspace that connects and the walls on the earth that disrupt. Enlightened by the example of those Golden Age Titans of thought and science, we may realize that only through adherence to fundamental values could we reach the imperative of global consensus. Professor Ahmed remains a staunch believer in that potential. Inspired by the philosophers of the Golden Age, he retains his faith in human nature and in the light of their spirit accepts the daunting challenge of charting a course for the future. We wish him Godspeed in his mission to spread knowledge and understanding.

Dr. Haris Silajdzic, Former Prime Minister
and Chairman of the Presidency of Bosnia Herzegovina

Professor Akbar Ahmed's writing always provides a roadmap to the global community on resolving contemporary societal issues. This book is vitally important as it arrives when society desperately needs to be enlightened about great saints and philosophers' mutual respect across history. It sends a powerful message supporting religious pluralism and challenges us as practitioners of multi-faith understanding and collaboration to promote further the core values demonstrated by these Golden Age philosophers. Every practitioner of multi-faith understanding must read this unprecedented discovery.

Dr. Mohamed Elsanousi, Executive Director,
The Network for Religious and Traditional Peacemakers

Akbar Ahmed, being the thinker that he is, has a special knack for providing a refreshing yet historical perspective to our modern-day crucibles, challenges stemming from the ill of our times, soullessness. Through Ahmed's adroit penmanship, as we travel through time in the transcendentalism of Islam, we are prodded to figure out at what point exactly we, as humanity, lost touch with the fundamental relationship with our soul that makes us who we are, distinct from other creatures. Ahmed does not stop there, as any good practitioner, as a man of immense professional experience, and as a statesman, he subtly alludes to ways through which we actually can mend that very relationship.

HE Dr. Merve Kavakci, Turkey's Ambassador to Malaysia

As a pandemic, racial injustice, serious political unrest and climate change ravage so much of our world, Ambassador Akbar Ahmed's latest book arrives like a healing balm. Using the Golden Age of Islam as an example par excellence, Ahmed shows how it is possible for people from many cultures to get along by using the "*ilm*-ethos", i.e. the love of learning and wisdom as advocated by the Quran. His knowledge of all periods of history up to and including the present-day is phenomenal. From the scholarly works of the ancient Greek philosophers such as Plato, to the great Muslim minds of the Golden Age such as Avicenna, to the atheistic ideas of present-day individuals such as Richard Dawkins, Ahmed synthesizes it all to show the way to a better future.

Ambassador Ahmed has been a bridge builder between the world's peoples and the world's religions all his life. Compassion is a central idea in all his works. It was while reading one of his previous books, *Islam Today*, over 17 years ago that I realized that my personal religious beliefs were coincident with those of Islam, leading to my conversion to Islam. Ahmed often speaks of the philosophers of the past, Renaissance Men, as being individuals whose intellectual pursuits were not limited to one specific area. I have long contended that he himself is a Renaissance Man whose ideas would be widely respected by the great philosophers of the past. We thank him for trying so mightily to show us a way out of the dilemmas of today's troubled world.

Dr. Wardella Doschek, Secretary / Treasurer,
The Muslim Women's Association of Washington, DC

Dr. Akbar Ahmed's work, in a fascinating way, bridges the natural progression and the universal connection of the major philosophers and their contributions to humanity up to the present. In experiencing the current challenges facing the world today, this body of work is very timely, underlining that the present is connected to and inherits the past. Philosophers, regardless of religion, have concluded that to be scientific they must be objective, and not base their work on identities of race, ethnicity, nationality, etc. but rather upon the universal human type that we all belong to.

Talib M. Shareef, President and Imam of Masjid Muhammad,
The Nation's Mosque and Professor at Global Oved Dei Seminary University

The retrieval of this humane, wise and generous tradition is a real necessity for us all. This book, from perhaps the most distinguished and versatile Muslim scholar in the English-speaking world today, brings out both the intellectual and the human qualities of the great souls presented here.

Dr. Lord Rowan Williams,
Former Archbishop of Canterbury and Master, Magdalene College, Cambridge

THE
FLYING MAN
THE GOLDEN AGE OF ISLAM & ITS CONTRIBUTION TO SCIENCE & PHILOSOPHY

AKBAR AHMED

Contents

Preface	xi
Introduction	1
The Objectives of our Study	5
The Philosophers of the Golden Age	19
Avicenna	22
Al-Ghazali	30
Averroes	41
Ibn Arabi	51
Maimonides	59
St. Thomas Aquinas	70
A Thought Experiment of the Abrahamic Faiths	75
The Abrahamic Elements of An Ideal Society	79
Conclusion: The Relevance of the Philosophers To Our Times	87
The Dark Clouds of Islamophobia	90
The Wisdom of the Past Masters	102
Endnotes	121
Bibliography	125

PREFACE

This small book is a humble offering to the reader, in the hope that it acts as a reminder of the religious scholars of the past and the rich universal legacy they have left behind. It by no means claims to be comprehensive; it is merely an introduction and an invitation for the reader to explore the scholars of that age for themselves. For my wife Zeenat and me, confined to our home in Bethesda in the strict COVID-19 lockdown in December 2020, when the number of American deaths came to 3,700 on one day, far beyond the loss of life on 9/11, researching for this book was an escape from the lugubrious daily stories of illness and death. It converted the obvious vulnerability both of us faced on account of our ages and medical conditions into a welcome period of thoughtful stimulation and spiritual contemplation. The mall and the multiplex may have been out of bounds for us, but we had Ibn Arabi, Al-Ghazali, and Maimonides inviting us into their world. The nobility of their thought and sublimity of their expression contrasted with the angry tones, braying and threatening, we heard all day on television. The lies, slander, and character assassination (Trump, according to those who were counting, had told over 30,000 lies and falsehoods in a "tsunami of untruths" since coming into office), the daily random shootings, the increasing number of suicides, the manifestation of overt racism, and the collapse of moral leadership were exacerbated by the rampant COVID-19 virus.

On the 6th of January 2021, when the daily deaths from COVID-19 had risen to over 4,000, large armed mobs stormed the Capitol building, smashing windows and brushing the inmates and police aside. Nothing like this had happened since a British army attacked the same building two centuries ago. The mobs were joined by disparate groups, including the shadowy QAnon, who believed that Trump was their champion, challenging a cabal of Satan-worshipping pedophiles who were conducting child sex trafficking and blood sacrifice. Confederate flags were spotted in the mob. Men with painted faces in ghoulish colors and some wearing Viking helmets, complete with horns, invaded the Capitol building and walked its corridors. They pushed into the Senate Chambers and mocked the offices of the high and mighty by sitting with their legs insolently placed on the desks of senior members. They had been encouraged and goaded by Trump. By the end, several lives, including that of a policeman, were lost. Late into the night, prominent Americans, clearly traumatized, commented on TV, their eyes glistening with tears. But had they been blind over the last four years of Trump's reign? He had scattered numerous clues in full view which pointed to this outcome.

There were more shocks to come as it was revealed that many of the rioters were themselves policemen accompanied by former servicemen. Some had come with intent to harm senior figures like Mike Pence and Nancy Pelosi, who had swiftly escaped to safety from their offices. For inciting the insurrection, Trump now faced impeachment and dismissal before his presidency ran out on the 20th of January. The D.C. Mayor declared a curfew, and there were rumors that the imposition of Martial Law was imminent.

On top of the other negativity, this was the last straw; it made me wince at the cruel irony that it was the vision of America the Beautiful, America the Brave, America the Compassionate, that had attracted us to come to the US in the first place. Engaging with the great philosophers of the past was thus an exercise that kept us sane and engaged. It was a magnificent escape from Donald Trump.

Nonetheless, nothing could diminish the ache that came from the lack of close contact with family and friends, especially our beautiful children and grandchildren—the girls in the UK and the boys in Washington, DC—so near yet so far. We were so proud of them, their integrity, and achievements, and although we talked daily on the phone, we worried for them, as parents do, for bringing them into this precarious world. We felt helpless and unable to reach out and touch them, to embrace them, and say to each one, "I love you." Once again, the philosophers came to our rescue. If nothing else, they taught us the power of faith, the belief in something bigger than us. They also reminded us how interconnected different parts of humanity are to each other, and how the world is shaped by the quest to know each other and find ways to live in harmony while reaching for the Divine, each in our own way. It reintroduced us to some of the most distinguished philosophers of the past and underlined the relevance of their ideas for our world today. We were reminded of those values that make us human and we aspire to in our finest moments: hope, faith, compassion, mercy, and the pursuit of knowledge.

I am grateful to the following for their assistance in the writing of this study. Even the dreadful coronavirus did not delay or dampen their enthusiastic support: Distinguished Professor Amitav Acharya, Zeenat Ahmed, Fakhri Al-Barzinji, Osama Al-Zain, Dr. Qibla Ayaz, Gary Berman, Rabbi Mendel Bluming, Dr. Roger Boase, Professor Michael Brenner, Dean Christine Chin, Wardella Doschek, Senior Associate Dean Carolyn Gallaher, Dean Emeritus Louis Goodman, Dr. Amineh Ahmed Hoti, Ambassador Dr. Merve Kavakci, Grand Mufti Husein Kavazovic, Frankie Martin, Mitchell Moskowitz, Professor Seyyed Hossein Nasr, Imam Talib Shareef, Dr. Haris Silajdzic, Professor Tamara Sonn, Lord Rowan Williams, and Sheikh Hamza Yusuf.

INTRODUCTION

Imagine a man created in a state where he finds himself suspended in mid-air, eyes blindfolded, and his hands stretched out tightly so that he cannot touch anything or feel his body. Although he would not know he had a body, he would still be aware of the existence of his "self" or "soul." The soul is therefore both distinct from and something more than the body. This was the conclusion arrived at by Avicenna, the Persian philosopher who lived in the tenth and eleventh centuries, in his "thought experiment" which has come to be known as the Flying Man or Floating Man. (For the purposes of this study, we will be using the globally popular names of the great philosophers of the past, for example, Avicenna for Abu Ali al-Husayn ibn Abd Allah ibn Sina, or Ibn Sina, and Averroes for Abu al-Walid Muhammad ibn Ahmad ibn Muhammad ibn Rushd, or Ibn Rushd.)

The Flying Man

Although Avicenna's Flying Man is one of the most striking images and experiments in the history of philosophy, not everyone is convinced about the validity of the thesis, citing a lack of credible evidence. For similar reasons, some have doubts about Plato's allegory of the cave and Nietzsche's theory of the superman. As scholars, we note the echo in purpose in the examples of scholars like Avicenna, Al-Ghazali, Plato, and Nietzsche, despite their differing cultural backgrounds and the times in which they were living. They all express the human search for truth and light, the desire to encourage and elevate the destiny of man, and remind us of the importance of knowledge and learning, even if some of these ideas are indirectly expressed.

Plato's allegory of the cave is one of the most celebrated thought experiments in Western philosophy. The plot is simple, but the lessons are profound. A group of prisoners have been chained in a dark cave and forced to stare at a wall. Behind them is a fire, and the shadows of the prisoners are cast on the blank wall. These shadows move about and appear to represent human forms. The prisoners are led to understand that this is reality. Eventually, one of the prisoners manages to escape from the cave and makes his way with great difficulty into the surrounding world over the ground. He is dazzled by the sunlight and the birds, trees, and bushes around him. He could easily leave his fellow prisoners to their fate, but his human impulse prompts him to go back into the cave to try to persuade them to escape and see the world outside. The reaction of his fellow prisoners is unexpected. They believe the shadows on the walls are reality and will not change their minds. At first, they argue with him and soon become angry and threaten violence.

INTRODUCTION

Our next example is that of the concept of the ubermensch or "superman" that comes from Nietzsche in *Thus Spake Zarathustra*. Although the concept has been widely misused and distorted, the idea is a worthy one. The ubermensch is simply a more evolved, more noble, and better version of ourselves. Nietzsche argued that man's evolution could not have stopped where it did and still needed to develop to fulfill his destiny; thus, the evolution of the superman.

We note that the contribution of a Muslim philosopher ranks alongside that of the A-list philosophers of history. Considering how broadly and unfairly Islam is associated with terrorism and mayhem, this may come as a surprise to some; in that case, other surprises await the reader who is unaware of the Golden Age of Islamic scholarship. As for Avicenna, we will return to him after I explain the purpose of this study.

THE OBJECTIVES OF OUR STUDY

The primary purpose of this study is to share information about a remarkable period of history, between the ninth and thirteenth centuries, often referred to as the Golden Age of Islam. We will examine some of the leading, but by no means all, philosophers of the Golden Age. By describing them as philosophers, we use the term "philosophy," *philo-sophia*, in the ancient Greek sense of the word, which means "love of wisdom." The figures we will discuss all admired wisdom and sought it through inquiry, research, and knowledge. They were thus true philosophers.

A study of these philosophers will be instructive in several ways that are both practical and spiritual. Philosophy then meant something else than how it is conceived in our time. It included astronomy, mathematics, and even medicine. The Muslim philosopher then justified his studies based on the Quran, which asks the faithful to look around the earth and up at the stars and wonder at the majesty and glory of God. The Quran, the philosopher maintained, virtually commands us to become philosophers. Secondly, the purpose of this book is to inspire those seeking knowledge about Islam and those who have a poor impression of Islam's capacity for scholarship. Thirdly, it is to engage with those scholars and commentators who deride Islam as a religion incapable of serious thought and one that promotes little besides anger and hatred. These people react defensively to the media depiction of Islam as backward, violent, and anti-intellectual. The gap between mainstream Islam and those in the community who wish to explore their faith in a more modernist or secular frame remains wide. There needs to be a viable method that allows different and contrary voices to be heard without resorting to fisticuffs and abuse. Fourthly, our study raises the issue of the treatment of scholars in the past and contrasts it with their plight in the present and the need for presidents and leaders of today, especially of the Muslim world, to cherish scholars and not to hound and persecute them. This exercise is also intended to promote a better understanding of, and between, the great faiths. Their points of similarity outweigh their differences as will be amply demonstrated in the chapter, "A Thought Experiment of the Abrahamic Faiths."

Information on these scholars is available and more eloquently and elegantly expressed in books, articles, and even videos. Therefore, my aim is to better understand Muslim society in the past and to extract lessons we can learn for today. My aim is not to further depress Muslim scholars who constantly bemoan the greatness of the past in contrast to the bleakness of the present but to point to what was achieved by fellow Muslims and what can be achieved again. In short, I seek to illustrate that there is nothing intrinsically keeping

The Objectives of Our Study

Muslim societies in a state of inertia and academic somnolence. As Muslims, they are commanded by the Quran and the hadith, or sayings of the Prophet Muhammad, peace be upon him, to acquire knowledge as part of their faith. There is a well-known hadith: "Seek knowledge even unto China." Our scholars who sought knowledge were what the Greeks called "peripatetic philosophers"; they were prepared to go to China to discover knowledge.

Facing questions of mortality with the COVID-19 pandemic creating misery and destruction all around me, I returned to these sages and in the process relearned their lessons for our times. It was an exhilarating process reacquainting myself with the great philosophers of the past. In this study, we will consider some of the major philosophers of the Golden Age, in particular Avicenna, Al-Ghazali, and the Andalusian Spanish philosophers Averroes and Ibn Arabi, who lived in the twelfth and thirteenth centuries. There were also non-Muslims whose work overlapped with these Muslim philosophers to mutual spiritual benefit. Among them, we could include the great Jewish and Christian philosophers of their time whose writings would inspire followers of their faiths up to our times – Maimonides and St. Thomas Aquinas, respectively.

While we restrict our study within the bounds of the Abrahamic faiths to maintain methodological focus, we know that research and the pursuit of knowledge have no bounds. The Golden Age of Islam produced scholars like Al-Beruni, a contemporary of Avicenna, who studied the non-Abrahamic religion of Hinduism. He was a polymath who mastered physics, mathematics, astronomy, and languages. He is said to have written 146 books. Al-Beruni was cast in the mold of our philosophers of the Golden Age. I have previously argued that, based on his impeccable research and rigorous methodology, which are clearly visible in his available works, he deserves the title of the "first anthropologist." A thousand years before Western "Indianists" like Louis Dumont and Adrian Mayer, Al-Beruni had given us a framework to study caste, kinship, commensal rituals, and *rites de passage* in Indian society. He mastered Sanskrit and spent several years living in Indian villages among Hindus. His book *Tahqiq ma al-Hind* or "The Investigation of India," popularly known as *Kitab al-Hind*, or "The Book of India," is the most authoritative source we have for Indian society a thousand years ago. Unlike our other star philosophers who lived in the western and central parts of the Muslim world, Al-Beruni worked in Ghazni, in present-day Afghanistan, in the court of the warrior-king Mahmud of Ghazni. Al-Beruni and Mahmud, scholar and king respectively, had famous clashes. To the wisdom and learning that these scholars had, we may add courage and integrity. There is the courage exhibited in facing the charging bull, and there is the other kind of courage in the face of a pandemic like COVID-19, with members of the family ill and dying, and yet showing the determination to carry on. Our philosophers exhibited courage of the latter kind.

The lives of these great scholars sometimes overlapped, while some were born shortly after the death of one of their number. Al-Ghazali was born two decades after Avicenna's death, and Averroes was born two decades after Al-Ghazali died. St. Thomas Aquinas was born two decades after the death of Averroes; Averroes and Maimonides died within a few years of each other. Ibn Arabi, it is said, spent time with Rumi in Damascus. Each one of them brings us closer to God, and each one of them shares the trials and tribulations they faced on the journey to discover the truth of God.

Cover of Al-Beruni's India. An English edition, London: Kegan Paul, Trench, Trübner & Co., 1910. 2 volumes.

The Flying Man

A thousand years is sufficient time to put distance between us and the subjects we are commenting on. But, by definition, while we may, with a degree of accuracy, record certain facts such as the year of birth and death or the titles of their main publications, there remain gaps in their lives, which may best be served by intelligent conjecture and prescient imagination. Only sometimes in history can we associate one individual as an appropriate representative of an entire age. We can thus confidently talk of the age of Shakespeare or Queen Elizabeth in England, or the Victorian age during the reign of Queen Victoria, and we remain confident that others know exactly what we mean. One individual sets the tone for and dominates the imagination of that period of history, becoming its very symbol and inspiring imitation, controversy, and debate. But imagine an era of history in which there were literally dozens of such individuals, each of whom we could have chosen to represent an entire age. Their achievements were spectacular and, studying them a thousand years later, I am in awe of them.

From Cordoba in the west to Bukhara in the east and Baghdad, Cairo, and Damascus in the center of Muslim civilization, the zeitgeist was defined by the pursuit of knowledge which engendered scholars and scholarship. In the west there were giants like Averroes, Ibn Arabi, Maimonides, and St. Thomas Aquinas. Al-Ghazali stoutly held the center. To the east there were also giants like Al-Farabi, Al-Beruni, Omar Khayyam, and Avicenna. There were many more scholars of note but for the purposes of our study, we are restricting the number. Such undoubted geniuses and in such numbers living within one cultural civilization has rarely been witnessed in human history. The nearest example was provided by Europe over half a millennium later, when England produced Francis

Bacon, Thomas Hobbes, John Locke, Isaac Newton, David Hume and Adam Smith, and the continent produced Voltaire, Baruch Spinoza, Jean-Jacques Rousseau and Immanuel Kant.

It is the urge in our times to categorize in an excess of taxonomic compulsion which reduces our scholars and philosophers into boxes that would have been meaningless to them. They were essentially free-spirited scholars following their intellectual curiosity and research wherever it took them. Sometimes it landed them in trouble, as with Avicenna. But the sum of their efforts and the direction of their lives conveys the philosophy of that time: knowledge must be followed by the scholars wherever it takes them. While we force our scholars into reductive and simplistic pigeonholes—Ibn Arabi for Sufism and mysticism, Al-Ghazali for mainstream formal Islam, Averroes for philosophy and the interaction with the Greeks, and Avicenna for medical research—we are aware that we are simplifying something that cannot be simplified. They were far more sophisticated and their knowledge was far too great to be contained and restricted in one narrow channel. Neither can we categorize them in terms of Shia versus Sunni, or in the context of Persian versus Arabian culture, or label them as fundamentalist and secular as we so blithely do today. Persian, for example, was not only a linguistic and ethnic description but also a cultural one, and it extended far beyond the boundaries of the Persian state. I believe not only did these categories and terms mean very different things to that society, but that it is a sterile exercise that can only prevent us from truly understanding the scholars of the past and their scholarship.

In their lives and work, these scholars, while faithful to their own religious traditions, reached far beyond their families, communities, and intellectual circles. Promoting understanding and compassion, they were "minglers" in the classic sense, as defined by Mughal Prince Dara Shikoh in his seminal study *The Mingling of the Oceans*.[1] The signs of this mingling are clear: Avicenna treated Muslims and non-Muslims alike with his medical expertise; Al-Ghazali admired Aristotle; Averroes spent a lifetime translating the Greeks; Ibn Arabi came to faith by seeing visions of Jesus; Maimonides tended to Muslims and non-Muslims, worked at the court of a Muslim ruler, and wrote in Arabic; and St. Thomas Aquinas used and cited the works of Muslim scholars like Averroes, Al-Ghazali, and Avicenna extensively.

Great as their reputations may be, the stories of these philosophers illustrate their humanity, and glimpses into their lives allow us to identify with them. Each one of them proved to be vulnerable and susceptible to the vagaries of fortune, which their grand titles and heavy reputations as the leading thinkers of their age could not protect them from. There is the fall from power and grace; there is nervous breakdown and eventual recovery; and we are acutely aware of the massive currents of history that swirl around them, threatening to destabilize and even destroy the societies within which they lived.

The Golden Age of Islam was a time of great intellectual and cultural achievement. It was also a time when some outstanding kings ruled both Muslim and non-Muslim lands. Among Muslims, there was Harun al-Rashid, the Abbasid caliph, Abd ar-Rahman III of Andalusia, and Saladin, the sultan of Egypt. Among Christians, there was Alfonso X of Castile, Roger II of Sicily, and Frederick II, Holy Roman Emperor. All of these rulers had an inclination to seek knowledge and promote it in their kingdoms. There was clearly a symbiotic relationship between the ruler and the scholar, with the latter invariably looking for patronage and support in order to be able to conduct his studies. It was widely known that Roger II would not sit on the throne out of deference until his Muslim advisor, Al-Idrisi, was seated.

It is notable that during the Golden Age of Islam, some Christian kings were influenced by Islamic learning and wisdom, and ruled with compassion, justice, and tolerance. They spoke Arabic, were guarded by Muslim soldiers, and showed respect for Islamic knowledge and culture. Their popular titles proclaimed their reputation as promoters of tolerance: King Roger II of Sicily was acknowledged as a great ruler who appreciated Muslim culture; Alfonso VI was known as the "Emperor of the Three Religions"; and Alfonso X The Wise was called "The Last Almohad Caliph" for his sympathetic attitude towards Muslims. Frederick II, the Holy Roman Emperor who was given the title of *stupor mundi* (wonder of the world), performed a feat extraordinary in the annals of international relations and diplomacy: in the midst of the Crusades, Jerusalem was handed over to Frederick II peacefully, by Al-Kamil, the King of Egypt and nephew of the legendary Sultan Saladin. Their relationship of mutual respect was cemented by reverence for scholars and scholarship.

Jewish and Christian scholars, like Muslim philosophers, have contributed significantly to scholarship, raising the standards of debate and discussion to unprecedented heights. They were all inspired by what I call the "*ilm*-ethos," a society's ethos of pursuing knowledge that transcended religious boundaries.[2] The level of discourse, the libraries, the royal patronage, and the high prestige attached to scholarship among Muslims encouraged them to pursue knowledge and inspired intellectuals living in Christian Europe. This pursuit of knowledge, or *ilm* in Arabic, is fundamental to Islam and drove Muslims to the heights of civilization and innovation during the Golden Age. Non-Muslims who engaged with Muslims and their philosophical debates surrounding the reconciliation of religious faith and Greek philosophy also shared this ethos. The rulers set the standards by stocking their libraries with an abundance of books and manuscripts. For example, the ruler of Cordoba, Al-Hakam II, was said to have possessed a main library with 600,000 books and manuscripts, and that was only one of the 93 libraries in the city. Meanwhile, Christian Europe's largest library had only 600 manuscripts. Rulers invited scholars from all over the world and personally attended and encouraged debate at the mosque after prayers. It was not uncommon to see a ruler sitting on the carpet surrounded by students and scholars in one corner of the mosque, earnestly debating various issues, perfectly symbolizing the *ilm*-ethos.

When mentioning the libraries of Andalusia, it is important to keep in mind that this region was still on the periphery of the Muslim world. There were even greater libraries in Damascus, Baghdad, Cairo, and Bukhara. The Grand Library of Baghdad, also known as the House of Wisdom, had acquired a mythical status as the greatest library in existence at that time. Its collection of books included translations of works from Greek, Persian, and Indian sources, and its facilities for scholars enjoyed the direct patronage of the ruling Caliphs of Baghdad, who took great pride in it.

Before we discuss the philosophers of the Golden Age, we need to point out that they were influenced by a rationalist school of Islamic theology that flourished in the capital Baghdad in the previous centuries between the eighth and tenth centuries. They were called the Mu'tazila. The name Mu'tazila reflects the origins of the group and derives from the Arabic word "to withdraw or retreat," in this case, from a theological position. The group later referred to themselves as "people of monotheism and justice," emphasizing divine unity (*tawhid*) and divine justice (*al-adl*). The name Mu'tazila was subsequently used by their opponents in a derogatory sense.

The debates conducted by the Mu'tazila now seem obscure and esoteric, and the intensity with which they were conducted appears baffling, but in their day, they were the center of heated controversy and a matter of life and death for the protagonists. Questions regarding the origin of the universe, the creation of the Quran (against the orthodox belief that it always existed), the nature of evil, and the relative importance of the Quran versus the Hadith (the sayings and doings of the Prophet Muhammad, peace be upon him) were fiercely debated. Members of the group grappled with the "problem of evil," reconciling an omnipotent God who is the embodiment of justice with the reality of evil in the world. Evil, therefore, arises from errors in human actions that result from "free will." The Mu'tazila believed that good and evil are rational categories and that knowledge is the "final arbiter" in distinguishing right from wrong, not always determined by revelation. According to the school of *kalam*, God's laws needed to be based on rational thought because reason, rather than "religious precedent," should determine what is accurate in religious practice. By the ninth century, the Mu'tazila had gained great power in Baghdad, the capital of the Abbasid empire, and were said to have influenced leading Muslim philosophers who followed them in the next centuries, like Averroes. The Mu'tazila had become powerful enough at court in Baghdad to have the influential Imam Hanbal persecuted and tortured. The public backlash against them led to the Mu'tazila losing a great deal of ground and being persecuted. The Mu'tazila continued to be influential among the later Umayyads, especially in Andalusia. Through their thinking and practices, the Mu'tazila had provoked the enmity of mainstream orthodox Muslims. These movements frequently split into separate streams, and while some were revived under different religious leaders with a different emphasis, others merged with larger groups; many weakened and faded away. Today, the term Mu'tazila is used by rival groups of Salafis to attack each other's credibility.

In setting the cultural and philosophical context of our main philosophers, it is time to point out the central importance of the Greeks in Muslim thinking during that period. The presence of Greek ideas in Islamic thinking had become a fact of reality and could not be ignored. Not only were Greek texts translated into Arabic, but their main works were thoroughly absorbed, and their arguments were engaged with and developed in different and original directions. Of the Greeks, Socrates, Plato, Aristotle, and Galen were the most popular, and among them, Aristotle had caught the imagination of the Muslims and captured their hearts. Muslim philosophers attempted to reconcile Aristotle with the Quran. European philosophers like Étienne Gilson have argued that Averroes was heir to the ninth-century Mutazilites who endeavored to reconcile Aristotle with the Quran. The problem for them was "How to think as Aristotle if we believe as Muhammad?"[3]

The combination of talents in one individual that these philosophers embodied would be precisely what came to be known as the Renaissance Man in Europe. Waqas Ahmed has defined such figures as polymaths.[4] It would be almost a thousand years later when science and the arts would be brutally cleaved into two distinct cultures on the assumption that they had little to teach each other. It was a loss to both. Today, philosophy is a greatly reduced and narrow subject from its heyday at the time of the Golden Age.

Imagine an individual, to take an example from our time, possessing the expertise of the immunologist Dr. Anthony Fauci, the religious scholar and philosopher Rabbi Lord Jonathan Sacks, the linguist Noam Chomsky, and the astrophysicist Neil deGrasse Tyson. That level of combined brilliance comes close to describing each one of the main figures, whether Avicenna or Ibn Arabi, discussed in this book.

In addition to their philosophical interests, many philosophers were also notable poets. Poetry gave these philosophers a special insight into human nature and an understanding of the human predicament. It kept them grounded, no matter how abstract and spiritual their philosophical flights were. The *ilm*-ethos and the cultural environment of the Golden Age ensured that the philosophers possessed a combination of disciplines that reflected a dazzling array of knowledge. They contributed to the practical application of learning; for example, several of them studied to become prominent medical physicians and chemists. They mastered algebra, algorithms, mathematics, and astronomy, and some even attempted flight. It is no coincidence that one of the first inventor-scholars to attempt flying was Ibn Firnas in Cordoba, who is said to have been in the air for about 10 minutes. A prominent bridge in Cordoba depicting huge wings to symbolize his achievement is named after him, as well as a crater on the moon. It is also no coincidence that many of the stars, planets, and 24 craters on the moon are named after Muslim scholars to honor them, including Averroes and Avicenna.

THE PHILOSOPHERS OF THE GOLDEN AGE

The Golden Age of Islam could be said to have begun with the rule of the Caliph Harun-al-Rashid (786–809 AD), the legendary Caliph of *One Thousand and One Nights*, when his capital Baghdad was acknowledged as the greatest city in the world with its unique House of Wisdom that contained knowledge from different world civilizations. If the Golden Age is assumed to have begun in Baghdad, it also ended in Baghdad when the Mongols sacked the city and massacred its people in 1258.

The Golden Age was characterized by both a prolific output of intellectual activity and raging public debates involving the philosophers, followed intently by sections of the general public. As can be imagined, each of the philosophers had much to say about the key issues of their time. They were like the superstars of their age and enjoyed devoted followings in a civilization that stretched broadly from Cordoba in

Andalusia to Bukhara in Uzbekistan. Their reputation travelled even beyond Muslim societies.

Despite the different times and places in which they lived, all of the philosophers we discuss in this study shared several things in common: they were born in one place and very often died in another; were child prodigies; wrote prolific and high-quality literature; were involved in controversies that very often resulted in attacks from fellow philosophers and theologians; were favorites of the ruler one day and targets of his wrath the next; and though they came to symbolize their respective religious communities, they also acted as ambassadors for dialogue with those of other religions.

The Greeks, who had already made deep inroads into Islamic thought in the previous centuries, came into their own in the Golden Age. It was sometimes difficult to see where Greek philosophy ended and Islamic theology began. Ibn Arabi, "The Greatest Sheikh," reflected this love affair with the Greeks when he addressed Plato as *Aflatun Elahi*, or the "Divine Plato". In *Madina al-Fadila*, Al-Farabi argued that the role of the philosopher was to offer guidance to the state. Here he was following Plato's *The Republic*; however, instead of Plato's philosopher-king, the Muslim state would be ruled by the prophet-imam. Al-Farabi wrote that the ideal state was the city-state of Medina when it was set up by the Prophet Muhammad, peace be upon him, who was not only the head of state but also received revelations about law from God. Al-Farabi, known as the "Second Teacher" after Aristotle, lived mostly in Baghdad in the ninth and tenth centuries and aimed to synthesize Aristotelian philosophy and Sufism, which influenced Avicenna.

As for Avicenna, he appeared to have absorbed Aristotle so fully and enthusiastically into his thinking and methodology

A 17th-century manuscript of Al-Farabi's commentary on Aristotle's Metaphysics. The Bodleian Library, University of Oxford

that his critics accused him of apostasy. It is therefore not entirely surprising that a later Muslim philosopher with theological confidence and credibility, uneasy at the inroads Greek thought had made into Islamic theology, had to stand up and say enough is enough. That task, as we shall see below, fell to Al-Ghazali, widely known as the Defender of the Faith or *Hujjat al-Islam*.

Al-Ghazali argued against the ideas of Avicenna and other Aristotelian Muslim philosophers called *falasifa*, such as the belief that the universe has always existed. The philosophers believed that demonstrative proof is superior to theological knowledge, which comes from revelation. Al-Ghazali rejected this position while still accepting some of the ideas of the Aristotelian-inspired philosophers. Al-Ghazali's acceptance of demonstration led to the successful introduction of Aristotelianism or Avicennism into Muslim theology. The writings of the philosophers and the Greek sciences were thus "naturalized" into the teachings of *kalam* (science of Islamic doctrine or Islamic methodology deployed in defense of Islam). Al-Ghazali's approach later influenced Averroes and through him, Jewish and Christian thinking.

The debates among philosophers and scholars at that time were deadly serious and centered around substantial issues. Three issues, in particular, agitated Muslim minds. The first was the nature of the universe. Did the universe always exist or was it created by the command of God? The second was about the nature of God. Did God know everything about everyone on earth all the time or did God follow events in a more general way? The question of resurrection after death was the third big issue. What happened to individuals after they died? Would they be resurrected and if so, what form would they take?

Aristotle argued that the universe always existed and did not accept the idea of resurrection in the traditional sense. In opposition, Al-Ghazali claimed that God created the world from nothing. Aristotle also believed in the inseparable unity of body and soul, and it was for this reason that he asserted that it was impossible for the soul to survive the death of the body. Against this, Avicenna, influenced by Plato, argued that the body and soul were two distinct substances. It was in illustrating this proposition that Avicenna put forward the thought experiment of the Flying Man.

◊ AVICENNA: "THE JEWEL OF THE EAST":
"THE MOST FAMOUS SCIENTIST OF ISLAM AND ONE OF THE MOST FAMOUS OF ALL RACES, PLACES AND TIMES"

As was usual among Muslim philosophers of the Golden Age, Avicenna memorized the Quran at an early age. In his case, he did so at the age of ten, and then went on to master philosophy, medicine, mathematics, and logic while still a young man. Avicenna absorbed the ideas of the Greeks, but he did not simply replicate them. Born in Bukhara, then a flourishing center of learning to rival Baghdad, Avicenna wrote the encyclopedic *Canon of Medicine* and *The Book of Healing*, which earned him royal patronage. His impact stems from the fact that he combined so many different intellectual traditions and forged them into one coherent frame within which to apply his knowledge, especially in medicine. Avicenna was also considered the most influential medical doctor of his time.

In discussing Avicenna's life, it is relevant to mention briefly the larger religious politics of his time. Avicenna, through his father, was suspected of belonging to the Ismaili order, a sect of Shia Islam that was known to have ties to a group dubbed "the Assassins," who proved to be a serious threat to the Sunni order through their policy of targeting Muslim rulers. One such target was Nizam-ul-Mulk, the patron of Avicenna. A powerful and successful administrator, he was the chief minister of the powerful Sunni Seljuk Empire. Nizam efficiently administered the provinces while balancing both the Turkish rulers with the Persian population, as well as Shia and Sunni Islam. He wrote an influential book on governance called the *Siyasat Namah* or "The Book of Governance." He created colleges with high standards called "Nizamias" and patronized educational institutions in Medina and Mecca. In the end, the Assassins succeeded in killing Nizam-ul-Mulk, though similar attempts on the life of the famed Sultan Salahuddin or Saladin, failed.

Avicenna saw himself as a philosopher synthesizing the thought of the Greeks, especially Aristotle and Galen, rather than an Islamic theologian tilting towards revelation and faith

The Flying Man

Left, a portrait of Avicenna dated 980–1037. Right, the opening decoration and invocation to Allah from a 16th century manuscript of Avicenna's Canon of Medicine.

to explain phenomena. Avicenna, like Aristotle, believed that the universe has always existed, an idea that challenged orthodox Islamic thought. In separating the soul and the body in his experiment, however, Avicenna departed from Aristotle, instead foreshadowing the dualism of Descartes's *cogito ergo sum* or "I think, therefore I am." Both the Persian and the Frenchman sought to establish that the mind's knowledge of its own existence proves its very existence and is therefore distinct from the human body. By further arguing that the soul is not destroyed when the body dies and is immortal, Avicenna was also following Plato on some key issues, particularly in regard to the body, soul, and afterlife. In doing so, Avicenna drew the further ire of more orthodox Muslims, especially the Islamic theologian Al-Ghazali, who lived in the eleventh and twelfth

A front page of the Siyasat Namah, the most famous work by Nizam al-Mulk, the patron of Avicenna.

centuries, and argued that anyone who denied the idea of physical resurrection was committing heresy.

Like other philosophers, Avicenna was an original thinker. Here are some of his scintillating ideas which had a widespread influence within and beyond the Muslim world:

The first is his famous thought-experiment of the Flying Man, mentioned at the start of this book. Second, his ingenious argument titled "The Proof of the Truthful" in which he set out to prove the existence of God. Contingent things exist but could have not existed or could cease to exist, like the universe which is contingent because it depends on something else for its existence. In contrast, God exists because he cannot *not* exist. He is the "necessary existent." Avicenna's thesis was picked up by Maimonides, St. Thomas Aquinas and others. Professor Peter Adamson calls it one of the key ideas in Islamic thought.

Third, his opinions as a physician on medical and health issues such as treating patients holistically, using psychology and other means to help patients recover were contained in his famous *The Book of Healing* and the *Canon of Medicine*. These were in vogue in Europe until the seventeenth century and are still used in the Muslim world. His ideas of quarantine to contain a pandemic were relevant to us in the face of the threat of the COVID-19 virus, which paralyzed so much of the planet.

Fourth, although Avicenna was attacked (most prominently by Al-Ghazali) for being overly influenced by the Greek philosophers, he was critical of Plato's ideas. Being an original thinker, he took certain ideas of Aristotle while rejecting others. Paradoxically, while Muslims condemned him for not accepting the central Islamic belief in the bodily resurrection of the dead, Christians reading his work in Latin appreciated his arguments, as they appeared in consonance with Plato's idea of an immortal soul.

Fifth, in addition to his scholarly work on philosophy, medicine, and his autobiography, Avicenna produced notable works of poetry. His poems were written in Arabic and Persian. The following verses are said to be those of Avicenna, although they are incorrectly attributed to Omar Khayyam:[5]

> From the depth of the black earth up to Saturn's apogee,
> All the problems of the universe have been solved by me.
> I have escaped from the coils of snares and deceits;
> I have unravelled all knots except the knot of Death.

Some scholars of Avicenna, even those like Professor Peter Adamson who are admirers of the philosopher, point out his failings, such as the fact that he was "pleased with himself," his partiality to alcohol, and his amorous dalliances.[6] When Adamson repeated his comment that Avicenna had a high self-regard, "enjoyed life," which included drinking wine, and had a "well-developed sexual capacity," he was reprimanded by a mildly irritated Melvyn Bragg. Would Adamson have preferred, said Bragg in his gentle way, Avicenna to have been more like the English and maintained "a stiff upper lip"?

Avicenna died in his mid-50s, which was below the average age of the other philosophers mentioned here. Writing several hundred books and pouring out poetic verses, moving from one location to another regularly and keeping one step ahead of public controversy, he had simply exhausted himself. His friends warned him to slow down his pace of life. He was aware that time was running out but he refused to change his ways, saying, "I prefer a short life with width to a narrow one with length." Sensing that his death was near, he spent his last days reading the Quran and abiding by its injunctions to do charity. Avicenna's life had not been without controversy. He moved from court to court to find security. The ruler of Hamadan in Persia imprisoned him for several months, and he escaped in disguise to Isfahan. Buried in Hamadan, rumors persisted that he was poisoned in the end.

Avicenna, in death more than perhaps in life, gets excellent press. Although some hailed him as *Hujjat al-Haq* or "Embodiment of Truthfulness" and *Natasha-e-Sharaq* or "The Jewel of the East," controversy and suspicion surrounded his work as many Muslims viewed his ideas as uncomfortably radical. His reputation has grown since his death. Dante placed Avicenna in Limbo; after all, he was not a Christian, but he was given special honor alongside Homer, Socrates, and Plato. George Sarton, the author of *The History of Science*, described him as "one of the greatest thinkers and medical scholars in history ... the most famous scientist of Islam and one of the most famous of all races, places, and times."[7] In the 2013 film *The Physician*, based on the novel with the same title, Avicenna is played by Ben Kingsley, the actor who played Gandhi in Attenborough's film *Gandhi*. In the Persian Scholars Pavilion, Vienna International Center, UNO City, there are statues honoring Avicenna, Al-Beruni, Zakariya Razi, and Omar Khayyam. His image is featured on banknotes in Tajikistan.

The support that Avicenna enjoys across ideological and political boundaries is illustrated by the fate of the imposing monument built in his honor in the city of Hamadan, Iran. Built by the Pahlavi dynasty in the early 1950s, it was feared that the Islamic revolution of 1979 could damage or alter its name. In fact, Ayatollah Khomeini himself admired Avicenna, and the monument and the square named after the philosopher remained untouched.

Professor Seyyed Hossein Nasr, one of the leading Islamic philosophers of our time and the author of many heavyweight books on Islam, including *Islam and the Plight of Modern Man* (1975), was particularly enchanted by Avicenna and Ibn Arabi, describing them in superlative terms.[8] Sitting comfortably in our home during the pandemic lockdown, while observing the required distance between us, we discussed Islamic philosophy over green tea in the cold month of November 2020. Outside, the air was dense with the threat of violence as the nation, eerily divided into two exact halves, both believing in opposite ideas of what it meant to be American in the wake of President Trump's refusal to accept his loss at the elections, reeled with uncertainty.

Professor Nasr recounted the story of when the Shah of Iran invited him to meet and hinted that he was thinking of the young Iranian scholar as a future Prime Minister. Nasr politely disabused the Shah of the idea, saying if he was required to give a lecture on Avicenna, he would do so happily, but being involved in politics was not his cup of tea. Professor Nasr, who is himself the author of over 50 books and 500 articles, reminded me that over 200 books of Avicenna have survived. Commentators estimate that Avicenna may have written double that. The scale of his achievement is mind-boggling.

Let me conclude with a reference to the controversial declaration by Al-Ghazali that led some people to believe Avicenna was an apostate. We will hear Al-Ghazali's side of the story below, but this accusation hung over Avicenna like a dark cloud and has still not completely disappeared. Some questions are raised that are not clearly answered. Was Al-Ghazali motivated by genuine Islamic commitment, professional jealousy, or sectarian zeal? We can never truly be sure. Perhaps there was a sectarian edge to Al-Ghazali's perception of

Avicenna, who was suspected of being an Ismaili on account of his father. Al-Ghazali himself was tasked by Nizam-ul-Mulk to challenge and expose the Ismailis. What we do know is that Avicenna's name was revived after the pandemic that the world faced in 2020 through the very notion of quarantine. His wisdom and skills as a medical physician once again came to the service of humanity.

◊ AL-GHAZALI: "PROOF OR DEFENDER OF ISLAM," HUJJAT AL-ISLAM

Al-Ghazali's significance lies in his resolution of the major divides that existed within Islam. He bridged the gap between mainstream, orthodox Islam and its more mystical side, broadly known as Sufism. The other divide was between Muslim philosophers who were excessively influenced by the Greeks and their alarmed critics who saw this as a threat to orthodox Islam. Until Al-Ghazali definitively resolved the issue, Muslim theologians and philosophers worked within two opposing Islamic interpretations of Aristotle. One emphasized reason and argued that the position of both Aristotle and the Prophet of Islam was valid, with Avicenna being the most prominent philosopher supporting this position. The opposite view was represented by Al-Ghazali, who, while respecting Aristotelianism, nonetheless gave it a position subordinate to Islamic theology where they were in conflict. Al-Ghazali blamed Avicenna for not pointing out the inherent conflict that existed between Aristotle and Islam on some central issues. The controversy around creation was just one bone of contention. Al-Ghazali, while condemning Avicenna, nonetheless wrote about Aristotle in admiration, in particular mentioning four of his works: *The Generation and Corruption, Heavens, History of Animals,* and *Physics.* He appreciated

Aristotle's methodological approach to knowledge, which rested on concrete empiricism. Al-Ghazali added a spiritual dimension to Aristotle, but however great his fascination with Aristotle was, he made sure it did not venture beyond the boundaries of Islam.

The discussion about Greek influences on Islam was encapsulated in Al-Ghazali's devastating attack on Avicenna and Al-Farabi (although the real target appears to be the former) in *The Incoherence of the Philosophers*. While references to boxing and football in a discussion on philosophy may be somewhat unusual and even raise eyebrows, I deliberately select sporting metaphors to convey the brutal and gory Al-Ghazali takedown, which in its method and impact was a knockout as fatal as that of Muhammad Ali's in 1965, making short work of Sonny Liston in the first round of the world heavyweight championship fight, and as irresistible as Maradona's "goal of the century" against the English team in 1986. In his genius, and the deftness with which he could wield it as a weapon, Al-Ghazali was a master craftsman in his field just as Ali and Maradona were in theirs.

In *Incoherence*, Al-Ghazali meticulously sets up what he believes are the main arguments of his protagonists. He then systematically, with Aristotelian logic, goes down his list of twenty points, one by one, underlining those items that do not match with Islamic theology and law. The influence of Greek philosophy had reached a head by the time of Al-Ghazali. Muslim philosophers had taken to Plato and Aristotle enthusiastically, and it had become difficult for ordinary Muslims to identify the borders between Greek philosophy and Islamic theology. What Al-Ghazali did was rationalize those arguments based on reason which were compatible with Islamic revelation and point out those that were not. Matters of fact, for example, were not the subject of dispute. On Al-Ghazali's list of points that he saw as un-Islamic, three were the most serious and the Greeks differed from Islam on all three: the question of creation, the nature of God, and resurrection. It is precisely on these points that he takes philosophers like Avicenna to task. On all three, Al-Ghazali's position was the same as that of Maimonides and Aquinas. As for Avicenna, he stood with Aristotle on at least one of these issues and was ambiguous about the others. Al-Ghazali was not against Aristotle because he was a bigot and loathed the Greeks. In fact, Al-Ghazali made a point of expressing his esteem for Aristotle and even used the Greeks' method of logic and rationality in his arguments.

Those who call themselves Muslim and do not accept these points of Islamic belief, like Avicenna, are therefore guilty of heresy. There is no aporetic mystery here: it is a clear-cut case. There really is no counter argument. In religion, it is either this side or that of the line. Religion, especially the Abrahamic variety, does not allow for shades of gray or ambiguity. Faced with this situation, Avicenna was clearly in dereliction of his religion.

In correspondence with me, Sheikh Hamza Yusuf, one of the leading contemporary scholars on Al-Ghazali, asserted that Al-Ghazali did not focus on individuals or designate Avicenna or anyone else as *kafir* (disbeliever), but rather focused on ideas:

> *He never made specific takfir (excommunication) of an individual. He spoke about ideas. He doesn't declare him an apostate. He is heavily indebted to Ibn Sina. However, in his Tahafut, he refutes twenty key issues in peripatetic philosophy, three of which he considered involved disbelief: the eternity of the world, that God did*

not know particulars, and the rejection of bodily resurrection. He considers these beliefs to be kufr. But he does not designate Ibn Sina or anyone else as kafir.

Professor Tamara Sonn, another distinguished scholar of Islam, agreed with Sheikh Hamza Yusuf's position in correspondence:

He appends a fatwa at the end of The Incoherence which says that anyone who teaches any of the twenty positions he believes he has dismantled is a kafir, guilty of apostasy. He also condemned Ismailis as apostates, and many people believe Ibn Sina was Ismaili (his father is alleged to have been). But I don't know of any place where he directly did personal takfir on Ibn Sina.

When discussing Al-Ghazali, we need to remind ourselves that he lived a thousand years ago, at a time when Muslim civilization was dominated by Islamic traditions, values, and beliefs. To expect a theologian of the highest order like Al-Ghazali not to engage in an exercise to rationalize and document the basic features of his religion is unrealistic. He worked within the normative religious tradition, within its boundaries and parameters, using the symbols, language, and rhetoric of his religion to do what the other great Muslim philosophers were doing, that is, endeavoring to know God through worship, meditation, and scholarship.

Yet even a figure as eminent and widely respected as Al-Ghazali found the shoe on the other foot when, across the world in Cordoba, the Chief Qazi, along with other religious scholars, objected to the hadith cited in *Ihya Ulum al-Din*, Al-Ghazali's masterpiece, as false, therefore declaring it a heretical work. It was burned along with Al-Ghazali's other writings. The religious scholars of Cordoba declared

Al-Ghazali a non-believer. They recommended to the ruler that the books of Al-Ghazali should be banned throughout his kingdom in Spain and North Africa. On hearing this, Al-Ghazali is said to have cursed the Almoravid dynasty which, according to legend, resulted in the change of rulers from the Almoravid to the Almohad.

The *Stanford Encyclopedia of Philosophy*, in its detailed discussion of Al-Ghazali, takes the position that Al-Ghazali condemned those like the Ismailis who did not accept the three key points in his list of twenty as apostates:

> *In his function as a Muslim jurisprudent, Al-Ghazali adds a brief fatwa at the end of his Incoherence and declares that everybody who teaches these three positions publicly is an unbeliever (kafir) and an apostate from Islam, who can be killed.*[9]

The *Stanford Encyclopedia of Philosophy* connects Avicenna to Al-Ghazali and presents them in a unified Islamic frame:

> *On the Arabic and Muslim side, al-Ghazali's acceptance of demonstration (apodeixis) led to a much more refined and precise discourse on epistemology and a flowering of Aristotelian logics and metaphysics. With al-Ghazali, the successful introduction of Aristotelianism or rather Avicennism into Muslim theology begins. After a period of appropriation of the Greek sciences in the translation movement from Greek into Arabic and the writings of the falasifa up to Avicenna (Ibn Sina, c.980–1037), philosophy and the Greek sciences were 'naturalized' into the discourse of kalam and Muslim theology (Sabra, 1987). Al-Ghazali's approach to resolving apparent contradictions between reason and revelation was accepted by almost all later Muslim theologians and had, via the works of Averroes (Ibn Rushd), and Jewish authors, a significant influence on Latin medieval thinking (ibid).*

Al-Ghazali's argument of causation and the power of miracles was echoed by David Hume centuries later. Al-Ghazali maintained that fire will burn cotton, but it is not necessary it will always burn, as God's intervention can prevent fire. "The connection," Al-Ghazali argued in *Incoherence*, "between what is habitually believed to be a cause and what is habitually believed to be an effect is not necessary." Commentators have long made comparisons of David Hume's ideas of causation to those of Al-Ghazali. The Muslim philosopher, while pointing to the relationship of cause and effect, that is, of "necessary causation," nonetheless rejected it on account of the possibility of miracles. In contrast, Hume used his theory of causality to reject the possibility that miracles can occur.

In order to better understand Al-Ghazali, let us take a brief look at the factors that formed him. Al-Ghazali's father was a struggling wool merchant, but his admiration for scholars instilled in Al-Ghazali the thirst for knowledge. Al-Ghazali was a brilliant student and very quickly mastered a range of disciplines. Al-Juwayni, himself an outstanding scholar, said of him that he was an ocean in which you could drown. It was not certain whether he meant it as a compliment. He was acknowledged as an outstanding genius and given the highest post at the Nizamia in Baghdad, set up by Nizam-ul-Mulk himself in the capital of the Muslim world. "It was as if he were the Archbishop of Canterbury and the Regius Professor of Divinity at Oxford all in one," explained Islamic scholar Professor Carole Hillenbrand. She added, "He was only 33 when he got the job."[10]

Patronage, power, and scholarship; the links were clear. One of Al-Ghazali's earliest books was an attack on the Fatimid Ismaili rulers of Egypt, in which he chastises them for their beliefs and argued in favor of those of his patron, the ruler of Baghdad. Al-Ghazali, at the height of his official position at the university and proximity to power, came to realize that the methods and procedures, whether of the religious or political establishment alike, are little more than a facade. It took the restless genius of Al-Ghazali to see through the miasma around him and cut a path to the truth. He considered his own position untenable and his behavior intolerable. The doctors of his time diagnosed his ailment as "melancholia," what we today call a nervous breakdown. With the constant adulation around him and pressure to live up to his own reputation, Al-Ghazali was entering the phase we now know as "burnout."

At the height of his fame, Al-Ghazali had a breakdown. Addressing a large congregation at the mosque in Baghdad, he discovered he could not speak. He writes in his celebrated autobiography, *Munqid min al-Dalal* or "Deliverance from Error," it was as if God had "put a lock on my tongue." He could not eat or drink, and his friends were concerned for his health. The prescription was familiar: a change of scene was recommended. His life was about to change forever; if it was dominated by philosophy up until now, henceforth it would be dominated by spirituality and Sufism. Almost in complete secrecy, he gave it all up and left to follow the Sufi path, dressing, living, and behaving like traditional Sufis. He believed that unlike the formal scholars, it was the Sufis who knew the right path to God, and it was not through books and cold learning but through the beauty of the human heart and its emotions of love and compassion. Al-Ghazali had seen the corruption of the court and vowed never to work with rulers or their ministers. His wanderings took him to the tomb of Prophet Abraham in Hebron, where he repeated his vow. For more than a decade, Al-Ghazali traveled, prayed, and meditated, all the while seeking answers, even spending two years cleaning the floors of the Umayyad mosque in Damascus.

On his travels, Al-Ghazali came across a gang of brigands who asked to see what goods he was carrying. Books, the scholar replied. My life's work. We cannot conceal a smile at the image of Al-Ghazali, one of the most celebrated Islamic scholars of the entire Muslim world, pleading with a brigand to spare his books loaded on a donkey. The brigand laughed in the face of the scholar, who pleaded with the thief not to take away his books as these were his life's treasure. Gathering up Al-Ghazali's books, the brigand bellowed, "What sort of treasure is this that can be stolen so easily?" Here, wisdom encounters ignorance and is frustrated at its own limitations. But the encounter with the brigand had a lesson for Al-Ghazali. He realized what it meant: he needed to emphasize the inner journey and inner wisdom rather than rely on books and papers to find knowledge and impress people. Henceforth, his focus would be on developing his inner self. He would consciously offer his own spiritual transformation as an example for others to benefit from it.

Al-Ghazali emerged from his travels to write his magnum opus, *The Revival of the Religious Sciences* or *Ihya ulum al-din* in Arabic. The *Ihya* is contained in 40 volumes. Some of the seminal literature of our modern world is brief: *The Communist Manifesto* is a 23-page pamphlet which can be read within an hour, and the *Gettysburg Address* is only 272 words in length, which took Abraham Lincoln three minutes to deliver. In contrast, Al-Ghazali's *Ihya* is a massive exercise in reading, which precludes a wider readership with such pressure on time. We are therefore grateful to Sheikh Abdal Hakim Murad for completing the heroic task of reducing the 40 volumes to

An old page with marginalia from 'The Revival of the Religious Sciences or Ihya ulum al-din by Al-Ghazali.

40 hours of tape in a project called "Travelling Light" so that Al-Ghazali is more readily and easily available.

The *Ihya* covers all branches of knowledge. Al-Ghazali discusses rituals and worship and then explains why they are necessary. He goes into the details of how a good Muslim should behave and why that behavior is necessary. No scholar had gone into this territory in such detail. In *Ihya*, Al-Ghazali accuses scholars of hypocrisy and admits that he himself was in that category. It is a detailed and clearly laid-out guide to the faithful Muslim, underlining morality, virtue, and ethics. The *Ihya* covers a wide range of subjects based on human experience from the time we are born to the time we die. The author engages with high philosophic issues and also everyday ones. For example, how to eat a normal everyday meal: food must be chewed slowly and with gratitude, as it is meant to give you the energy through which you can know and worship God and His creation. You are unequivocally told to avoid pride or give way to anger. Backbiting is especially condemned and equated to the eating of the dead flesh of the person being maligned. There are instructions on how to wash for ablutions or wudu before each prayer. The *Ihya* is the indispensable guide for the pious Muslim and remains, a thousand years later, the gold standard for them throughout the world.

Perhaps the scope and significance of Al-Ghazali's intellectual depth in reconciling Islam with Greek philosophy and Sufism with mainstream orthodox Islamic thought within the Sharia and religious law is not fully realized. Al-Ghazali also made a seminal contribution to Islamic law and the interpretation of the Sharia. He not only examined the law in detail but explained why it was necessary and what function it provided. No scholar had done this before him on this scale and in this depth. In addition to his vast theological output, he wrote letters with great insight, which are extant. His poems reveal a highly intelligent, affectionate, and warm individual.

It was said that the gates of *ijtihad* or innovation were closed after Al-Ghazali, as change was no longer needed and explanations no longer necessary. His exhaustive learning as an orthodox preeminent scholar and his intense personal experiences as a wandering Sufi made his arguments impregnable. Al-Ghazali urged us to be "present with God," arguing that once a person is present before God, they notice God's creation and become truly sentient. Al-Ghazali also warns against the dangers of a superficial and outward understanding of Islam. He is scathing about the blind acceptance of faith. He is widely admired in the Muslim world and there are mosques and colleges named after him. Al-Ghazali also passed away like Avicenna in his mid-50s, a relatively young age. As in the case of Avicenna, this was perhaps also a case of sheer exhaustion. His life was a constant struggle which also involved extensive and hard travel. Al-Ghazali worked tirelessly and produced, according to him, "more than 70" works, although scholars like Sheikh Abdal Hakim Murad estimate he had written over 200 significant books.

The favorite readings of the last great Mughal emperor Aurangzeb were the writings of Al-Ghazali; the favorite readings of Aurangzeb's ancestor, the inclusive and tolerant Mughal emperor Akbar, were those of Rumi. Al-Ghazali, like most philosophers, is not easily comprehensible for those who are not scholars of philosophy. But thanks to the untiring efforts of some outstanding contemporary scholars, his thought is available across a wide range of easily-digestible media forms accessible online such as videos, podcasts, and other materials. Sheikh Hamza Yusuf, Tamara Sonn, Sheikh Abdal Hakim Murad, Frank Griffel, and Aisha Gray

Henry have contributed significantly to the understanding of Al-Ghazali. The excellent BBC Radio 4 series, *In Our Time*, with Melvyn Bragg, has discussed Al-Ghazali and other philosophers of the Golden Age which are available on YouTube. There is a marvelous illustrated book and video called "Imam Al-Ghazali for Kids" produced by Aisha Gray Henry.

For Sheikh Abdal Hakim Murad, Al-Ghazali was "the greatest mind of Islamic civilization" who was "venerated as a saint in his last years."[11] Al-Nawawi, the thirteenth-century Islamic jurist and scholar, said of Al-Ghazali's *Ihya* that if all the books on Islam were lost and *Ihya* survived, that was sufficient.

◊ AVERROES: "THE ISLAMIC SCHOLAR WHO GAVE US MODERN PHILOSOPHY"

Ibn Rushd, or Averroes, widely known as the "Father of Rationalism," was not impressed by Al-Ghazali's condemnation of Avicenna and other like-minded philosophers in *The Incoherence of the Philosophers*. Al-Ghazali argued that philosophers needed to have a grasp of the ideas of philosophy before attempting to challenge them. He made it clear that he had no objection to the various branches of philosophy such as physics, astronomy, or mathematics. His complaint was with metaphysics because he believed that the philosophers writing about the subject did not use logic, which they employed for the other subjects.

Averroes' response came in the form of a dialogue with Al-Ghazali to refute his arguments. Averroes was at his acerbic best: "To say that philosophers are incoherent is itself to make an incoherent statement." His title, *The Incoherence of the Incoherence* contains a direct response to Al-Ghazali. He explained that Al-Ghazali's attack on the philosophers was erroneous because his criticism was of Avicenna's thinking, who had misinterpreted Aristotle. By blaming Avicenna for the failings of philosophy, Al-Ghazali was doing an injustice to the subject, and especially to Aristotle.

As with his other writing, Averroes' aim was to create harmony between faith and philosophy, between Aristotelian philosophy and Islam. For Averroes, Aristotle was correct while the Quran was also the eternal truth. His book was not generally well-received by Muslims and barely made a dent in mainstream Islamic thinking. However, it is worth pointing out that Al-Ghazali's approach, which had been to reconcile reason and revelation, had been widely accepted by Muslim scholars and then through Averroes and Jewish theologians made an impact on wider Christian society and its thinkers.

Averroes' predecessors such as Avicenna partially succeeded in solving this difficult problem by crowning natural theology and leaving the door open for the supernatural light of revelation. Averroes believed that there was no conflict between true philosophy and theology even though philosophy founded on demonstrative knowledge produced more certitude. The truth, he argued, cannot contradict the truth. His book *The Agreement of Religion and Philosophy or Decisive Treatise* for Gilson is "a landmark in the history of western civilization."[12] In his *Decisive Treatise*, Averroes analyzed the relationship between philosophy and religion. He argued that philosophy needed to be considered an Islamic science and therefore to be studied by Muslims. He again underlined the importance of a non-literal reading of the Quran and the compatibility between Aristotelian philosophy and Islam. While agreeing with some of the work of his predecessors, especially al-Farabi and Avicenna, he also took them to task where he thought their thinking was fallacious. He rejected, for example, Avicenna's argument attempting to prove the existence of God as the Necessary Existent.

Averroes had been educated in the school of hard knocks: he began service under the Almohads with a whiff of suspicion that ended in ignominy and dismissal. Earlier in his career, he was already in Marrakesh when the ruler of the Almohad dynasty died and his son succeeded him. The new Caliph, Yaqub Yusuf, aggressively promoted education among his people. Early in his reign, the new Caliph's minister, Ibn Tufayl, himself a notable scholar and author of the famous novel *Hayy ibn Yaqdhan*, another example of a thought experiment, introduced Averroes to the ruler. The Caliph asked the young scholar whether the universe always existed or was created. It was a dangerous question because if the scholar gave the wrong answer, he would be out of favor with the Caliph. Averroes was cautious and avoided an answer until he was sure of the Caliph's opinion on the matter. Impressed by his grasp of philosophy, the Caliph offered him a place in his court.

Averroes would hold different important positions in the king's court, including that of physician and judge. But most significant for our purposes, the Caliph commissioned Averroes to work on a translation of the Greeks, in particular, Aristotle, Plato, and Galen. Averroes went to work on the Greek philosophers with enthusiastic commitment. His translations of Aristotle took three forms: Firstly, there was the straightforward translation; secondly, a translation with the paraphrase alongside it, and thirdly, commentary and comment.

Although Averroes is known as a philosopher, his work in medicine was groundbreaking. His *General Principles of*

Title page from a Latin edition of Colliget, or Al-Kulliyat fi al-Tibb, Averroes' main work in medicine, 1530

Medicine, Al-Kulliyat Fi al-Tibb, was used for teaching in European universities. This was a medical encyclopedia that described various diseases. He noted that a patient could not contract smallpox a second time and explained the reasons. His observations on blood circulation in the human body preceded the pioneering medical work of William Harvey, just as his writing on microbial life preceded Louis Pasteur. He is the first scholar in medical history who explained the function of the retinal layer and its importance to the eye and eyesight itself.[13]

Averroes attempted the difficult task of riding two horses with strong temperaments at full gallop: reason and revelation. He argued that both were different but came from the same stable, as it were. Philosophy was a product of the human mind while religion came from revelation. It was a turbulent ride, and Averroes soon found himself thrown off both horses. In the meantime, he had antagonized members of the religious order and the public who had begun to suspect that his teachings were in contradiction to those of Islam. He further alienated his critics by arguing that while only the philosophers could understand the true meaning of the Quran, the rest of society could best understand the Quran by accepting it literally. For Averroes, the Quran is a poetic approximation of the truth; in order to understand it, the text must be "interpreted" by those best suited to do so, in short, the philosophers of Islam. With this, Averroes was entering controversial territory. He agreed with Aristotle that the universe had always existed, arguing that there is nothing in the Quran to contradict this. This went against the normative opinion in Muslim society.

Averroes' overt admiration of Aristotle also antagonized fellow Muslims. When the Almohads made attempts to become more liberal, public pressure forced them to retreat. Averroes was a prominent victim and fell from grace. He died on 11 December 1198 at the age of 72 in Marrakesh and was buried there. Later, his body was brought for burial in the family cemetery in Cordoba. *General Principles of Medicine, The Decisive Treatise, The Incoherence of the Incoherence, Primer of the Discretionary Scholar, Long Commentary on Aristotle's Metaphysics, Commentary on the De Anima of Aristotle*, and *Commentary on Plato's Republic* are considered his most important books.

The cause of the downfall of Averroes had, as often happens in such cases, an obscure beginning. The philosopher was brought down by Venus, the Roman goddess of love and beauty. Averroes had been accused of *shirk*, one of the most serious breaches of faith in Islam as it suggests an association with God. Idolatry or associating anything with God is a major sin in Islam and derives from the primary teachings of Abraham. Translating a Greek philosopher, suspected to be Aristotle, Averroes was quoted as saying, "the planet Venus is a Deity." His critics pounced on this and accused him of blasphemy. It was the time of the Almohads and society was hyper-sensitive to issues of theology. The Caliph heard the evidence against Averroes and accepted the accusation against him. His books were burnt, his writings banned, and the ruler banished the philosopher from his court to Lucena, a Jewish village near Cordoba. Thus began the woes of Averroes.

Looking back on his catastrophic fate, I find it difficult to accept the accuracy of the accusation against him, considering that not only Averroes but his father and grandfather were Islamic judges. Averroes himself would hardly have made such a fundamental error as to suggest that an inanimate object like a planet could be an Islamic deity. It is more likely that the jealousy of his colleagues and courtiers motivated them to plan and execute his downfall. They seized on this opportunity and exploited it to the full.

The business of *shirk* can be highly controversial and dangerous for a Muslim. Take this example from 1993 when the BBC six-part television series *Living Islam*, based on my book *Discovering Islam*, was broadcast. One episode had me praying in Bukhara at the shrine of Baha-al-Din, the venerated founder of the Naqshbandi order. He was and is considered one of the most influential Muslim scholars and saints of Central Asia. Subsequent rulers expanded the complex of schools and colleges around his shrine. It was said that a visit to the shrine in Bukhara was the equivalent of performing the pilgrimage to Mecca.

After the episode was broadcast on the BBC, a delegation of religious leaders in Cambridge rang me and requested to see me. They expressed their admiration for my work and said the community respected me, but they had a bone of contention to pick with me. I invited them for tea and they arrived at my Cambridge home and expressed their dismay and objection to that particular scene. They said I was committing *shirk* because I was praying to a stone. I disagreed and explained that I was simply praying as Muslims do all over the world for the soul of the person buried in the grave, in this case, the saint. At that point, the call to prayer sounded on a watch one of them had, and they said they would like to pray. We had some sheets placed on the carpet of the living room, moved the TV against the wall, and, led by their religious leader, we prayed together. When we finished and were still seated on the floor, I said loudly to the leader of the prayer group that he and his companions had just committed *shirk*. They were surprised and began muttering objections. I pointed to the television set straight ahead of them. I saw you as did everyone in this room, I said, praying to the television

Summa Theologica, 1596, 'Summary of Theology', often referred to simply as the Summa, the best-known work of Thomas Aquinas

set, an inanimate object. Was this not *shirk*, I asked? They said that was absurd. I said it was as absurd as your thinking that I was praying to a stone. They quickly said their goodbyes after that. It was the last I heard from them.

I asked Dr. Qibla Ayaz, Chairman of the Council of Islamic Ideology of Pakistan, about the influence of our philosophers. He said, "Al-Ghazali has great influence on the Muslim mind; Ibn Rushd has been terribly ignored." While Averroes may have made a limited impact on the Muslim world, it was a different story with the non-Muslim parts of Europe. St. Thomas Aquinas was so deeply influenced by Averroes that he referred to him 503 times in his magnum opus *Summa Theologica* and referred to him throughout his work as "The Commentator". Aquinas, of course, was not a blind imitator of Averroes. While accepting many of the Muslim philosopher's arguments, he also disagreed with him. Aquinas, in turn, influenced and continues to influence the Catholic Church. Aquinas and Averroes were considered the two greatest Aristotelians of the twelfth and thirteenth centuries. Both were seriously interested in reconciling metaphysics and religious orthodoxy. What Averroes and other Muslim philosophers gave to Aquinas was an ocean of learning from which to pick and choose, reject and accept, enhance and develop ideas within a Christian framework.

The influence of Averroes on Aquinas' *Summa Theologica*, especially its opening parts, is clearly visible. So too are Averroes' discussions of God's existence, His attributes, His creation of the world, free will, and predestination. The similarity in content, method and philosophic direction of argument in understanding the Divine is remarkable. At least on a philosophic level, there is a notable degree of harmony between the Muslim philosopher and the Christian saint.

European scholars used Averroes' translations of the Greeks, especially Aristotle. His arguments reconciling science and reason with faith and belief were widely adapted by religious scholars and leaders within their own traditions. Averroes's writings were translated into Hebrew and Latin and were extensively studied over the next few centuries. Christian priests were so alarmed by his popularity in European schools of philosophy that in 1210, the Council of Paris banned teachings of Aristotle's *Natural History* and Averroes' commentary on it. Other religious centers followed but found it near impossible to check the work of Aristotle and Averroes effectively.

The followers of Averroes' ideas were called "Latin Averroists." Frederick II, the thirteenth-century Holy Roman Emperor, ordered that the work of Averroes be taught at the universities of Bologna as well as Paris, then the leading university in Europe. Muslim scholars, especially Averroes, were also to be studied in the new university that Frederick created in Naples, known today as the University of Naples Federico II. The emperor emphasized the importance of reason and logic in research and scholarship. Raphael, the Renaissance artist, included Averroes in *The School of Athens,* his celebrated painting of the greatest thinkers of history, which included Socrates and Plato in the foreground. There is a statue honoring Averroes prominently displayed in Córdoba and a crater on the moon named after him. Robert Pasnau, the American philosopher, summed up Averroes' impact on the West by describing him as "The Islamic scholar who gave us modern philosophy."[14]

◊ IBN ARABI: AL-SHEIKH AL-AKBAR OR "THE GREATEST SHEIKH"

Ibn Arabi, the celebrated Sufi, mystic poet, and philosopher, was born in 1165 in Murcia, Spain, and died in 1240 in Damascus. He was hugely influential during and after his lifetime. Renowned as al-Sheikh al-Akbar, or the "Greatest Sheikh or Master," he was widely believed to be a saint.

When he was still a young man, Ibn Arabi was very aware of the pluralist and inclusivist trends in Andalusia and met Jewish and Christian teachers. He was not as interested in the formal teachings of the religions as with what comes from intuition and the heart or, as he called it, *Kashf*, to reveal, disclose, or unveil. In Andalusia, where society had produced a number of outstanding Sufi sheikhs and teachers, many of them women, Ibn Arabi absorbed mysticism. One of his Sufi teachers was a tambourine-playing nonagenarian woman called Fatima Ibn al-Muthanna who told him, "I am your spiritual mother."

Ibn Arabi's spiritual journey is said to have begun when, as a teenager, he was spending an evening with friends and, as he raised a glass of wine, he heard a voice taking his name and admonishing him, "Oh Muhammad, you were not created for this." Startled and disconcerted, Ibn Arabi ran to the cemetery where he is said to have spent several days. During this time, he had visions of meeting the major Abrahamic prophets, Moses, Jesus, and Muhammad. These figures shared with Ibn Arabi the secrets of the universe. Jesus, in particular, resonated with the young Ibn Arabi who saw him as "the first teacher," "the first guide to the path of God," and "friend." Following the example of Jesus, Ibn Arabi decided to live in austerity and, like St. Francis of Assisi, gave up his worldly possessions. Ibn Arabi embarked on a journey from which he would not return, in search of the eternal mysteries of the universe. This would become his life's mission.

Ibn Arabi's father, noticing the change in his son, brought him to meet his already established friend, Averroes. Averroes was believed to have asked to meet the young Ibn Arabi because of his reputation. On meeting Ibn Arabi, Averroes appeared to be overcome with emotion and was visibly moved. Let us hear the story from Ibn Arabi cited in his work, *The Bezels of Wisdom*:

> *I was at the time a beardless youth. As I entered the house, the philosopher rose to greet me with all the signs of friendliness and affection, and embraced me. Then he said to me "Yes!" and showed pleasure on seeing that I had understood him. I, on the other hand, being aware of the motive for his pleasure, replied "No!" Upon this, Ibn Rushd drew back from me, his color changed, and he seemed to doubt what he had thought of me. He then put to me the following question, "What solution have you found as a result of mystical illumination and divine inspiration? Does it coincide with what is arrived at by speculative thought?" I replied, "Yes and no. Between the Yea and the Nay the spirits take their flight beyond matter, and the necks detach themselves from their bodies."*[15]
>
> *At this, Ibn Rushd became pale, and I saw him tremble as he muttered the formula "There is no power save from God." This was because he had understood my allusion... After that, he sought from my father to meet me in order to present what he himself had understood: he wanted to know if it conformed with or was different from what I had. He was one of the great masters of reflection and rational consideration. He thanked God that in his own time he had seen someone who had entered into the retreat ignorant and had come out like this—without study, discussion, investigation, or reading.*[16]

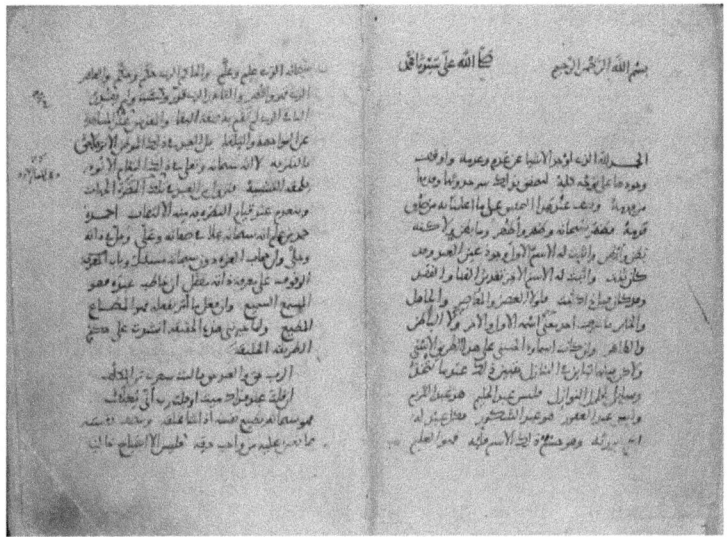

Opening pages of the Konya manuscript of The Meccan Illuminations or Al-Futuhat al-Makkiyyah, handwritten by Ibn Arabi between 1203 and 1240.

There is another anecdote that connects the two at the end of Averroes' life. On the philosopher's death, when his coffin, precariously tied on one side of a donkey with the books written by him on the other side for balance, approached the burial site, Ibn Arabi was said to have said, "On one side the Master, on the other his books! Ah, how I wish I knew whether his hopes had been fulfilled!"

In 1198, on the strength of a vision, Ibn Arabi set out on a journey to the East. During his travels, he had many mystical encounters which he detailed in his writings. Claude Addas in his *Quest for the Red Sulphur: The Life of Ibn Arabi* states that Ibn Arabi burnt several stages of a mystic's journey into one great leap by acquiring knowledge all at once. Nonetheless, Ibn Arabi did not abandon his plans to travel. He spent the latter part of his life traveling the centers of learning in the

Muslim world where he produced some of his most celebrated works.

On arriving in Mecca, Ibn Arabi received "a divine commandment" and began work on his magnum opus *The Meccan Illuminations* or *Al-Futuhat al-Makkiyyah*, which stretches over 37 volumes and has 560 chapters that cover his personal experiences and spiritual observations. It is 15,000 pages long. In *Futuhat*, Ibn Arabi explains we are only created to know and worship God; there is no other purpose. Ibn Arabi emphasized that Islam had not come to divide religions but, by incorporating the earlier teachings of the prophets, to unify worship of the Divine. His later book, *The Bezels of Wisdom*, is considered his masterpiece. His collection of love poems, *The Interpreter of Desires* or *Tarjuman al-ashwaq*, and his mystical commentary drew the anger of some of the scholars who forbade the reading of his works, while others elevated him to the ranks of saints. The depth of his poetry and the prolific nature of his output are astonishing. After Mecca, he traveled to Egypt, Anatolia, and Baghdad. As with so much of Ibn Arabi, the story of his supposed meeting with Rumi is shrouded in some mystery. The two mystics are said to have met in Damascus, but that remains conjecture. Ibn Arabi concluded his long pilgrimage in Damascus where he is buried, and, by the time of his death, saw his fame established throughout the Muslim world.

According to Professor William Chittick, a respected scholar of the mystic, Ibn Arabi produced some 850 works, of which 700 are said to be authentic. His main books are: *Al-Futuhat al-Makkiyyah*, *The Meccan Illuminations*; *Fusus al-Hikam*, *The Bezels of Wisdom*; *Tarjuman al-Ashwaq*, *The Interpreter of Desires*; and *Ruh al-quds*, *The Holy Spirit in the Counseling of the*

Soul, part of which is translated as *Sufis of Andalusia*. His *Diwan* is a collection of 5 volumes of poetry.

Ibn Arabi, like other advanced mystics, lived between several worlds which he made his own: between this and the other world, the conscious and the subconscious, and the real and the mystical. His writing method was to use poetry and prose, metaphysics and mysticism, and theology and autobiography. In his visions, he saw and was inspired by the beloved holy figures of Jesus and the Prophet of Islam. The role of women in inspiring Ibn Arabi throughout his life is also to be noted. Not only was one of his teachers a woman, but he advocated the role of women in teaching and even in leading the congregation in prayer. His claims to have talked with God, of having befriended the prophets, and walked on water elevated him in the eyes of many to the rank of the "greatest saint." Others were angry and baffled. They would be further aggravated to know that Ibn Arabi met Nizam, a beautiful, virtuous, and intelligent young girl in Mecca and believed she was his muse in writing his masterpiece *The Meccan Illuminations*. Ibn Arabi subsequently wrote another book as a commentary to explain that the beloved is simply the name of God. *The Bezels of Wisdom*, written in the latter part of his life and considered by many as his most important work, is a summary of his teachings and mystical beliefs, dealing with the prophets and divine revelation. *Bezels* was inspired by a vision in Damascus which Ibn Arabi describes in the preface: "I saw the Apostle of God in a visitation... He had in his hand a book, and he said to me, 'This is the book of the *Bezels of Wisdom*; take it and bring it to men that they might benefit from it.'"

Ibn Arabi describes the relationship between God and human beings as a great powerful white light that flows through a prism and is then refracted in countless colors that represent human beings. Those different colors reflect the white light of God. Man is thus merely a reflection of God and exists to reaffirm God's existence. But by being, Man provides a testament to the nature of God as the Essence. Creator and creation, the relationship validates each other, and the whole is suffused with love. One demands unqualified worship and the other the recognition of a special status in the order of things. One is all-knowing and all-powerful, and the other is created as God's deputy from whose ranks comes the *insan-i-kamil*. It is a tightly woven relationship, and its loosening sets the individual adrift. In that case, God, who does not need Man to exist, loses nothing, but Man, who is created in the image of God, loses his very raison d'être.

Among his most significant spiritual contributions are the concepts of the "perfect man" or *insan-i-kamil* and *wahdat-al-wujud* or the Unity of Being. For the former, Ibn Arabi cited Abraham, whose destiny and devotion are tied to God. He also described Jesus and Moses as perfect men. But the primary perfect man is Muhammad, the proof of God and path to God.

It is the complex and controversial concept of *wahdat-al-wujud* that still fascinates scholars. Creator and creation, worshiper and worshiped, and in Sufi parlance, the lover and the beloved, meet in the concept of *wahdat-al-wujud*. Ibn Arabi, who himself does not use this key concept in Islamic mystic tradition, explains the Essence of God as Wujud. God is not an essence. He is the Essence; the only Essence. There is no other. Nothing exists except for the Essence. Everything else is in relation to the Essence and derives its existence from *Wujud*. Worshipers are like mirrors reflecting the blinding radiance of the Essence. As God is the object and man the worshiper, if there was no God, there would be no creation. Thus, reuniting with God allows man to be reflected in the glory and goodness of God. Ibn Arabi's concept of Unity of Being made an impact wherever Muslims lived and whatever their professions. Prince Dara Shikoh was influenced by Ibn Arabi, and his own seminal work *The Mingling of the Oceans* reflects the central philosophy of Ibn Arabi.

Ibn Arabi described himself as a *Wali* (friend of God) and the seal of the *Walis*, keeping in mind that this simply means "friend" and Ibn Arabi is referring to himself as the *Wali* or friend of the Prophet Muhammad, peace be upon him, who in turn is the seal of the prophets. Ibn Arabi's critics saw such statements as proof of his arrogance and, along with his more controversial concepts such as *wahdat al-wujud*, made him a target of their wrath.[17]

Ibn Arabi was uniquely placed as the scholar who spent half his life in the West and half in the East to build bridges between the different traditions of both and thus bring them closer together. Ibn Arabi, in all his many literary expressions, emphasized the essential universalism of Islam. Everything he wrote, he asserted, was inspired by the Quran. He wrote down in detail the Sufi tradition, which was essentially oral, and thus preserved it for history. Ibn Arabi's visions continued as he traveled, and during his lifetime, he had established the significance of mystical and transcendental approaches to the divine, bypassing the legalistic and formalistic channels. He also brought Sufism into the mainstream in a more dramatic way than had ever been done before. Like many scholars of the time, he was acutely aware of Islam's predicament in being assaulted by the Mongols from the east and the Crusaders from the west. He watched the inexorable loss of Muslim prestige and power in the Iberian Peninsula. The fall of Córdoba, which for centuries had been the glittering capital of Muslim Andalusia, took place when Ibn Arabi was still alive, and he saw the Reconquista of the Iberian Peninsula gathering irresistible momentum. It was an augury of things to come.

Sufism was Ibn Arabi's legacy and gift to Islam, which gave the religion the capacity to survive some of the hard blows it was to receive in times to come. On my travels with the BBC while filming the *Living Islam* series in the early 1990s, I discovered that the Muslims of Central Asia maintained their faith under the brutal Soviet steamroller, which had set out to exterminate all signs of religion by falling back on Sufi methods and remembering God internally. In a small community outside Bukhara, I met a former Soviet soldier wearing the regimental long coat. He had served in the Soviet army, and his broad chest was covered with medals displaying the hammer and sickle. I found him instructing his grandson to recite the Quran through the practice of *zikr,* or the chanting of the names of God, in the Sufi tradition. Old women sat around the young lad, some on the ground, and wept uncontrollably. I was aware of something significant taking place. They were grateful that they had survived the Soviet nightmare and had been able to preserve their faith. The old soldier explained that it was the Naqshbandi tradition of *zikr* that had saved his community from the dreadful period of the Soviets who had set out to crush all forms of religion. Islam had survived by using the Sufi methods of faith. Here was evidence of the success of Ibn Arabi centuries after his death.

◊ MAIMONIDES: "FROM MOSES TO MOSES, THERE HAS NEVER BEEN ANOTHER MOSES"

There were notable parallels between Averroes' career and that of Maimonides. Both were quintessential citizens of Andalusia. Both wrote in Arabic. They both used reason and logic in appreciating faith and argued for the compatibility of the two. Their books were burned by members of their own community. They were exiled by the same dynasty. Averroes never recovered, while Maimonides flourished. Maimonides promoted the work of Averroes among his students. Today, both are recognized in the ranks of the greatest philosophers of history, while their critics are lost in obscurity.

Maimonides, or Rambam, a Hebrew acronym for "Rabbi Moses Ben Maimon", was born in Cordoba in 1138 and was a contemporary of Averroes, a fellow Cordoban. After largely living in peace and prosperity for four centuries in what is commonly referred to as the Golden Age for the Jewish community, the Almohads, a new dynasty from North Africa, took control of Andalusia and launched an offensive against the Jewish community, forcing them to choose between conversion, migration, or death. Synagogues and Jewish centers were destroyed, and Jews found themselves forced to wear special clothing. The father of Maimonides, then a teenager, Rabbi Maimon ben Joseph, was a respected elder and judge in the Jewish community. The family found itself on the run, first taking shelter in Fez and later relocating to Palestine and eventually arriving in Cairo. Maimonides wrote his celebrated note of consolation, *Epistle on Martyrdom*, suggesting that those who converted to Islam forcibly should maintain their faith, even if privately.

The wrath of the Almohads was not restricted to the Jewish community. The splendid city of Medina al-Zahra, built on the outskirts of Cordoba as a symbol of the culture, civilization, and prosperity of Andalusia, was destroyed by the Almohads as a show of their disapproval. Even Muslim philosophers with a reputation as great as that of Averroes were not spared. Averroes had to flee Cordoba and was only allowed to return shortly before his death. The image of one of the greatest philosophers of Islam at his lonely burial scene, as described above by Ibn Arabi, with his coffin on one side of a donkey and his books on the other to balance the corpse, is one of the most poignant in the history of philosophy.

What the Almohads did to the Jewish community was unusual in the broader historical context of Jewish-Muslim relations over the centuries. What was more usual was Maimonides's life in Fustat, a suburb of Cairo, which was home to a relatively small yet thriving Jewish community. The trauma of escaping from Spain to North Africa, masquerading as a Muslim, and then the tragedy of losing his beloved brother David, tested Maimonides to his limits. He was now looking after David's family as well as his own and needed to raise funds to support them. These personal difficulties did not dissuade Maimonides from attempting the ambitious project of summing up Jewish law and theology to offer the average Jew a practical guide to living as a good and moral believer. While his sources were rabbinical teachings, he also relied on Aristotle and Muslim philosophers like Avicenna, Averroes, and Al-Farabi.

In outward form, language, and culture, Maimonides had absorbed Muslim civilization. His typical day in the Sultan Saladin's court was always full, after which he hurried home to treat awaiting patients. Often, there would not even be

An autograph fragment of Maimonides' Guide for the Perplexed in Judeo-Arabic.

time for a meal before attending them. His success in society can be gauged from the fact that his son and grandson both succeeded him as Chief Rabbis of the Egyptian Jewish community.

The life of Maimonides resembles that of the Muslim philosophers we are discussing: intense creativity and serious, life-threatening challenges. Like them, Maimonides was a man of genius in several disciplines such as philosophy, religious law, and medicine. The titles of his books were as sharp as theirs: *The Guide for the Perplexed* as against Al-Ghazali's *The Incoherence of the Philosophers* and Averroes's *The Incoherence of the Incoherence*. His life took him from one part of the world to another; from living on the run in a cave at one stage of his life to serving in the royal court in Cairo at another.

The disruptions in his life had left the young Maimonides traumatized. He would have a love-hate relationship with Muslims for most of his life. In spite of this, Maimonides continued to reach out to the Muslim community and was a revered figure in Muslim society. His Muslim name was Abu Imran Musa ibn Maymun ibn Ubayd Allah or "Servant of Allah." It is reported that Maimonides' children and grandchildren rejected elements of his teaching and philosophy and some of them adopted certain Sufi practices.

In spite of the tumultuous life he led, he successfully created his most ambitious work and magnum opus, the code of Jewish religious law (or the Halakha), which is called the *Mishneh Torah* or "The Repetition of the Torah," considered the book of knowledge and its guide and commentary. Just as Al-Ghazali was called the "Defender of the Faith," Maimonides, on the basis of his works, is considered one of the greatest rabbis of all time.

Maimonides emphasized the role and thought of Abraham, who lived among polytheists but gravitated towards monotheism and rejected idolatry. Abraham emphasized monotheism and the belief that God created the universe and embraced all creation. Maimonides championed the concept of "negative theology," that is, understanding God through what He is not, as the best way to attempt to understand the true nature of the Divine. God is transcendent, all-knowing and all-powerful, while man is made in God's image and lives to realize that ideal. Maimonides also emphasized the distinction between the soul and the intellect, which are both pure. He also pointed to the body, which is "base," dealing with physical and material matters. Maimonides' life in Cairo allowed him to enjoy a relatively secure and stable environment after his dangerous and turbulent journey from Spain and through North Africa.

Maimonides argued that to practise one's faith correctly, knowledge and intelligence are essential, while ignorance must be eliminated. It was an argument Socrates used in discussing democracy, suggesting that only educated people who understand the ramifications of a democratic form of government should participate in it. He took much of Jewish scripture as allegorical and metaphorical, which other rabbis did not always agree with. His use of the word "perplexed" in the title of one of his most important books refers to the intelligent man who tries to understand and find a balance between inherited rabbinical law and the world around him. As a true philosopher, Maimonides first identifies the problem of existence and then illustrates how to move ahead to overcome it.

With reference to the main philosophical questions that interested Muslim philosophers, Maimonides believed that the soul and the body, while distinct, are still unified, with the former holding sway over the latter. The soul is divided into five parts: the nutritive part, the perceptive part, the imaginative part, the appetitive part, which is concerned with emotions and sensations, and finally, the rational part, which involves the capacity to interact with metaphysics. In *The Guide for the Perplexed*, Maimonides sets forth his views on the creation of the universe, which essentially reaffirms the traditional Jewish view on creation. Examining theories laid out by Moses, Plato, and Aristotle, Maimonides rejects Aristotle's argument that the world is eternal, instead championing Moses' view that the world was created by God out of nothing. Maimonides does write that Plato's view of a world created with pre-existing matter provides an acceptable alternative.

Maimonides was influenced by Aristotle, Al-Farabi, Avicenna, and Averroes, a fact he acknowledged. A towering Judaic figure, he was also quintessentially a product of the age of the *ilm*-ethos. Like our other great philosophers of that time, Maimonides emphasized logic, rationality, knowledge, research, and, above all, piety in his writings.

Yet there was also Jewish opposition to his ideas and philosophical approach—for example, Rabbi Solomon of Montpellier in France instigated church authorities to burn *The Guide* as heretical. Maimonides's views on resurrection received criticism from many rabbis and Jewish scholars of his period. In his *Treatise on Resurrection* (1191), Maimonides argued that the belief in the resurrection of the dead was a fundamental aspect of Judaism, and that on the issue of resurrection, Jews should not merely interpret Jewish scripture as allegorical.

In his work, Maimonides explored the righteous figures of Jewish history. He was inspired by Moses, who he saw as being closest to a perfect man, having both revelation and knowledge, but he also admired Aristotle and his writing on ethics and virtue. Maimonides provided a theological charter and framework for being a good human being, writing for two Jewish audiences—the individual but also for the larger community.

Maimonides emphasized the importance of philosophy in finding the best of human society, defining the subject in broad terms in the *Guide*: "The person who wishes to attain human perfection should study logic first, next mathematics, then physics, and, lastly, metaphysics."[18] The writing of Maimonides contains a stark beauty that shines with the light of integrity and wisdom. "Truth," he wrote, "does not become more true by virtue of the fact that the entire world agrees with it, nor less so even if the whole world disagrees with it."[19]

When I requested Professor Michael Brenner, a leading scholar of Judaism, to comment on my study, especially on the parts relating to Maimonides, he replied, "It is beautifully written and gives so much insight into a topic which indeed has tremendous relevance today." Brenner further commented on cross-cultural comparisons involving Maimonides: "It is interesting that, perhaps similar to Islamic thought in the period, Rambam's thought was also challenged during and after his lifetime, and many Jewish thinkers thought him heretic. The most influential thinker after him, Ramban or Nachmanides was rather critical of him and over the next few centuries it was mystical thinking and not his rational philosophy that dominated Jewish thought. In fact, while he was celebrated as the author of the *Mishne Torah*, his *Guide for the Perplexed* was banned by many communities for centuries and printed only late. There were even those who claimed that the two books could not have been written by the same person."

Rabbi Hillel the Elder was asked centuries before Maimonides to define the essence of Judaism while standing on one leg. "Do unto others as you want them to do to you," he said, enunciating what in effect is a universal Golden Rule. That is the essence of the Torah, the sacred text; the rest, Hillel said, is commentary.

Keeping Hillel in mind, I was interested in what Maimonides had to say about the subject of the other. Curious about the commentary of Maimonides on the matter, I asked my friend Gary Berman for sources. He kindly introduced me to his friend Rabbi Mendel Bluming, himself an admirer and scholar of Maimonides. I enquired of Rabbi Bluming whether Rambam has any guidance on the matter. "He absolutely does, Ambassador Ahmed," Rabbi Bluming replied. "I will find the exact citations and send them over to you." The Rabbi was true to his word. The following information is based on his research which he shared with me.

"The following is from Rambam's *Mishne Torah*, which is Maimonides' encyclopedia of Jewish Law, Chapter 10, Paragraph 12 of the laws of Kings. He writes that any non-Jew who lives in your land needs to be treated with respect and kindness, as the verse states in Deuteronomy, Chapter 14, Verse 21, 'to the sojourner in your gates you should give them food and kindness.' We should visit their sick, bury their dead, and sustain their poor, and that is the path of G-d about whom it says that G-d is good to all and bestows kindness to all of His creatures in Psalms, Chapter 145, and it says that the paths of the Torah are paths of peace and pleasantness in Proverbs, Chapter 3."

"In the laws of Kings, Chapter 9," Bluming continued, "Maimonides says that anyone who accepts basic laws of morality from all nations of the world (no murder, adultery, establishing a court system, etc.) has a place in the world to come. So, Judaism does not believe that paradise is reserved only for Jews. In his book of *Kinyan*, Chapter 9, paragraph 8, he says that those who adhere to the laws of the Torah are to be compassionate upon all, and that is the trait of G-d, and we are commanded to be similar to G-d. Anyone who is compassionate upon others, G-d will have compassion upon him as it says in Deuteronomy, Chapter 13, Verse 18."

"In the laws of Kings chapter 11," noted Bluming, "Maimonides praises the Muslims (and Christians) whom he says brought the idea of redemption and of adherence to God's laws far and wide so that this idea is known to all of mankind, paving the road for the entire world to be aware of and accept these concepts of serving our Creator." When I requested Rabbi Bluming to explain the reference to "Ismailites," the word used in the original, he replied, "He is referring to the Prophet Muhammad, who brought about a worldwide awareness of subservience to G-d."

Studying Maimonides, we note how close Jewish and Muslim thought is on some central issues of their faiths: the definition and position of God, the centrality of Abraham and the importance of Moses, the rejection of idolatry, and the need to create a better world where people could live good lives and worship God. In his method of teaching, Maimonides underlined the need to avoid getting tangled up in the weeds and to keep the big picture in mind. For that, he stressed the importance of learning and knowledge. He is influenced by the Greek-influenced Muslim philosophers, and Maimonides himself is influenced by Aristotle. Maimonides is constantly balancing theology with practical common sense. He talks to us directly as a great teacher.

Maimonides is both a gateway and a bridge: he is a gateway for the Jewish people into the understanding of Judaism, and a bridge between Muslims, Christians, and Jews. He thus remains in an extraordinarily relevant position a thousand years after his death. He is buried in Tiberias in Israel, and his grave on the shores of the Sea of Galilee is a popular pilgrimage site. His gravestone reads, "From Moses to Moses, there has never been another Moses." There are many stories which are now part of folklore about how his bones were brought from Egypt and buried here. There is a story about the Bedouin tribes who stopped the funeral procession in order to extract payment and then, realizing whose procession it was, hung their heads in shame because of the reputation of the man who, without payment, treated them and other patients when they were ill.

Maimonides was the most celebrated rabbi to emerge from Spain during the Golden Age of Islam, but there were other notable figures such as Rabbi Moses de Leon. Leon is widely believed to have composed the celebrated *Zohar*, which is a collection of rabbinic teachings reflecting the mystic aspect of Judaism, or Kabbalah. *Zohar*, which means "splendor" or "radiance," is considered the foundation of Kabbalah. Kabbalistic knowledge is said to have been given to Moses by God on Mount Sinai, and some scholars trace it back even further to Adam. The *Zohar* explains the relationship between the unchanging eternal God, the Infinite, and the mortal finite universe that is God's creation, and includes commentary on other fundamental issues relating to Jewish theology such as the nature of God and the origin and structure of the universe. The *Zohar* has been the center of discussion and controversy but is acknowledged as containing the essence of Jewish mysticism. Today, Kabbalah is known internationally and has attracted celebrities like Madonna, Roseanne Barr, and Mick Jagger.

I asked Mitchell Moskowitz, a scholar-administrator at my university who assisted me on this project, about Kabbalah. "I'd simply say it's Jewish mysticism," he replied. "Kabbalah is definitely not mainstream and is therefore not well understood by the majority of Jews, including myself. This is mostly attributed to the significant percentage of American Jews who are not especially religious or well-versed in Jewish theology and history."

Let us give the last word about the Golden Age and the role of Maimonides in it to the late Rabbi Lord Jonathan Sacks, himself one of the greatest rabbis of our times. In a 2015 interview with me, he described the exchanges between the religions going on at the time as "Convivencia," meaning coexistence, a term Spaniards still use to describe this period in Spanish history:

> *This period of al Andalus and under benign Muslim rule was one of the most, not only one of the most benign, but one of the most intellectually and spiritually creative in all of the Middle Ages. What had happened was that you had these extraordinary Muslim scholars who had recovered the classical tradition of the Aristotelians and Neoplatonists, and they were the first people in Europe to do so. They lifted Europe out of the Dark Ages. They then had an enormous impact on figures like Moses Maimonides, the greatest rabbi of the Middle Ages, whose philosophy, and almost every aspect of his work, was influenced by and stimulated by Islam. His creation of this magnificent legal code was inspired by Sharia codes. His formulation of the principles of Jewish faith was*

inspired by the fact that Muslim thinkers had done this wonderful presentation of Islamic faith. So, it spread from Islam to Judaism. It then spread to Christianity through Maimonides and influenced a figure like Aquinas. So, you have Islam leading Europe out of the Dark Ages.

◊ ST. THOMAS AQUINAS: "SAINT THOMAS IS AN AUTHENTIC MODEL FOR ALL WHO SEEK THE TRUTH"

St. Thomas Aquinas' name has grown with time, and many myths were attached to him to illustrate his spirituality. He was said to have levitated and seen the Virgin Mary in a vision. He emphasized that good ideas must be accepted from whatever their source and that reason was compatible with faith. He was clearly enchanted by the great Muslim philosophers like Averroes, Al-Ghazali, and Avicenna and Jewish philosophers like Maimonides. His extraordinary scholarship and character earned him sainthood. His writings, like his magnum opus *Summa Theologica*, "Summary of Theology," written with the beginner in mind, and the hymns he composed, are still in use. There are nuggets of wisdom and common sense in the writing of Aquinas, pithily expressed. "Thus, the sun," observed Aquinas in *Summa*, "which possesses light perfectly, can shine by itself; whereas the moon, which has the nature of light imperfectly, sheds only a borrowed light." He is considered one of the greatest theologians of Christianity.

The significance of St. Thomas Aquinas was that he established within the Christian philosophical tradition the idea that reason and revelation could co-exist harmoniously. The influence of Averroes on his thought was apparent: he cited the Muslim philosopher extensively in his writings. Ernest Renan, the distinguished French Orientalist scholar of the origins of early Christianity, wrote St. Thomas Aquinas was "the first disciple of *The Grand Commentator* (Averroes). Albertus Magnus owes everything to Avicenna, St. Thomas owes practically everything to Averroes."[20]

Pope John Paul II, who was himself elevated to sainthood, spoke of "the dialogue" that Aquinas "undertook with the Arab and Jewish thought of his time" and announced that: "[T]he Magisterium has repeatedly acclaimed the merits of Saint Thomas' thought and made him the guide and model for theological studies... The Magisterium's intention has always been to show how Saint Thomas is an authentic model for all who seek the truth. In his thinking, the demands of reason and the power of faith found the most elevated synthesis ever attained by human thought, for he could defend the radical newness introduced by Revelation without ever demeaning the venture proper to reason."[21]

Pope Benedict XVI was, like St. John Paul, an ardent admirer of St. Thomas Aquinas:

> *"In his encyclical Fides et Ratio, my venerable predecessor, Pope John Paul II, recalled that 'the Church has been justified in consistently proposing St. Thomas a master of thought and a model of the right way to do theology' (No. 43)."*
>
> *It is not surprising that after St. Augustine, among the writers mentioned in the Catechism of the Catholic Church, St. Thomas is quoted more than any other—at least 61 times! He was also called the Doctor Angelicus, perhaps because of his virtues and, in particular, the sublimity of his thought and purity of his life.*
>
> *In short, Thomas Aquinas showed that a natural harmony exists between Christian faith and reason. And this was the great achievement of Thomas who, at that time of clashes between two cultures, when it seemed that faith would have to give in*

to reason, showed that they go hand in hand. Insofar as reason appeared incompatible with faith, it was not reason, and so what appeared to be faith was not faith since it was in opposition to true rationality. Thus, he created a new synthesis which formed the culture of the centuries to come.[22]

Pope Francis, the present Pope, declared Amoris Laetitia (The Joy of Love) is in continuity with previous Church teaching and "follows the classical doctrine of St. Thomas Aquinas."[23] In short, the most authoritative voices in the Catholic Church are unanimous in declaring St. Thomas Aquinas the best role model and scholar.

Because St. Thomas Aquinas is such a towering figure in the Catholic Church, he tends to overshadow other notable contemporaries. Apart from Aquinas, there were major Christian preachers in the Dominican order of the Catholic Church influenced by Muslim philosophers, especially Averroes, Al-Ghazali, and Avicenna. Among the most prominent was Bishop Albertus Magnus, who, like Aquinas, was also canonized as a saint by the Catholic Church. Although Aquinas is better known than his teacher Albertus Magnus, Albertus was considered one of the greatest philosopher-theologians of the Catholic Church and hence his popular name Albert the Great. Dante in his *Divine Comedy* frequently mentions Albertus, along with his pupil Aquinas, as the great lovers of wisdom in the Heaven of the Sun. Albertus' references to Al-Ghazali exceeded those of his pupil Aquinas. Albertus was also influenced by Averroes, the great translator, and scholar of Aristotle. The ideas of Aristotle, filtered through and infused with Islamic thought, were thus transmitted to European theology and thought.

At least two other Christians deserve a mention: Marguerite Porete, the female mystic, and author of *The Mirror of Simple Souls*, who was burned at the stake for heresy by the Church in France, and Meister Eckhart, who was tried by the Pope for heresy and had several of his writings declared heretical and dangerous. Eckhart, a successful German member of the Dominican order of the Catholic Church, and a popular speaker before he fell out of favor, was influenced by Porete, but his main inspiration came from Aristotle, Aquinas, Maimonides, and Averroes.

Eventually, Eckhart's concepts and influences landed him in trouble with the Church. Eckhart used the German word "*grund*," ground, earth, or reason, which describes the essence of God as a key concept. God's reality emanates from the *grund*. The soul and God are one. My *grund* and God's *grund* are, therefore, the same. For Eckhart, God was the essence and God's relationship with the soul, one reflecting the other to the point of unity, pointed to the two fusing into one. Eckhart argued that God is goodness, and as we are good, we share and become part of God's goodness. God is also wisdom, truth, and compassion, and "insofar as" God has these attributes, the same principle, which he called "the Quantum Principle," applies. As God is everything, and the soul nothing, it does not need to exist and is therefore in a state of what the Sufis call *fana* or annihilation. Some of Eckhart's main ideas on Christian mysticism remind us of Ibn Arabi's notion of *wahdat al-wajud* or the Unity of Being. Eckhart combined philosophy, theology, and mysticism in exhilarating but controversial ways to understand God.

Eckhart's recognition by the Catholic Church, and that of Porete, is long overdue. A thorough study of this area where different religions and civilizations meet and interact is much needed. Studies of this period are perhaps neglected because Europe prefers to label the Golden Age of Islam as the Dark Ages and therefore not worthy of attention.

A THOUGHT EXPERIMENT OF THE ABRAHAMIC FAITHS

In this section, we will explore the similarities in the larger spiritual visions of the three Abrahamic faiths through a thought experiment. Taking three of the most renowned religious scholars from each faith—Maimonides for Judaism, Al-Ghazali for Islam, and St. Aquinas for Christianity—from the Golden Age, we will place their representative statements defining their faith in random order, without indicating the authorship. The aim of this experiment is to illustrate the close proximity of the ideals, values, aims, and objectives of the Abrahamic religions. Setting aside their respective particularistic rituals and symbols, the core essence of the faiths is remarkably similar: the belief in an omnipotent and invisible God, the prophets who bring down His message in sacred texts, and the restrictions and commandments prescribing certain things while forbidding others. Below are three sets of quotations from the writings of our three sages. Can the reader identify who said what?

- *"We must love them both, those whose opinions we share and those whose opinions we reject, for both have labored in the search for truth, and both have helped us in finding it."*
- *"Grant me, O Lord my God, a mind to know you, a heart to seek you, wisdom to find you, conduct pleasing to you, faithful perseverance in waiting for you, and a hope of finally embracing you."*
- *"Three things are necessary for the salvation of man: to know what he ought to believe; to know what he ought to desire; and to know what he ought to do."*

- *"The foundation of all foundations and the pillar of wisdom is to know that there is a Primary Being who brought all existence into being."*
- *"The judgments of the sacred text do not bring vengeance to the world, but rather bring mercy, kindness, and peace to the world."*
- *"Teach thy tongue to say 'I do not know,' and thou shalt progress."*

- *"All of a man's happiness is in his being the master of his ego, while all his suffering is in his ego being his master."*
- *"Four traits lift a person to the highest ranks, even if their works and knowledge are little: forbearance, humility, generosity, and good character. This is the perfection of faith."*
- *"The biggest barrier between you and God is you."*

The answer is: the first set of quotes is from Aquinas, the second from Maimonides and the third from Al-Ghazali. In the end, the greatest works of these sages, Maimonides' *Guide*, Ghazali's *Ihya* and Aquinas' *Summa*, have the same purpose and even use the same method in pursuit of it: to put forward the strongest and clearest arguments to worship God.

If you belong to one of the Abrahamic faiths, or even a non-Abrahamic one, and have negative ideas about other religions, you may look at the wisdom contained in these quotations and say these represent our civilization and culture. They may even evoke feelings of pride as you assume the quotations originate in your religion. But assessed objectively, you would be hard pressed to match the quotation with the correct author precisely because the similarity of the content, and even the language of the quotations, demonstrate that they are shaped and formed by original sources that are themselves reflective of one another.

While we recognize what is similar between the three Abrahamic faiths, Islam had unparalleled influence in this Golden Age, which necessitates an examination of the key features of Muslim society at the time. I also wish to draw attention to the fact established by our thought experiment that these features also reflect the values of Judaism and Christianity.

THE ABRAHAMIC ELEMENTS OF AN IDEAL SOCIETY

Considering the broad similarity of the Abrahamic faiths, can we extrapolate general principles from the work of the past masters to identify those features that form an integral part of an ideal society? We know that ideal societies rarely, if ever, exist or even come up to the expected standards that exist in the imagination. The Abrahamic philosophers, like the Greeks before them, grappled with the idea of how best to create the conditions for an ideal society in which humans flourished, a state that the Greeks called *eudaimonia*. Al-Razi, another great Muslim polymath of the Golden Age who lived in the ninth and tenth century, summed up the message of the Quran as one central formula: to worship God and to do service to His creation.

While I will be using Arabic Islamic names for the pursuit of knowledge, the imperative to be kind and compassionate and to live a life of piety, are all features of human behavior to be found in the other two Abrahamic faiths and indeed in the other great faiths too.

What the past masters whom we have discussed previously possess is a curiosity that is on constant display in their writing. They strive towards their objective of acquiring knowledge to find the best path to the Divine. They travel, often to distant sites, they face adversity and tragedy, they observe, they interact with people and places, and they record. This kind of curiosity, backed by the urge to research and inquire, is an aspect of modern civilization and its endearing aspect; but as our material shows, it does not originate in nor is it exclusive to modernity.

It is curiosity and intellectual restlessness that motivates even an establishment figure like Al-Ghazali to give up his high position and spend years wandering in the company of Sufis in search of answers. In the end, Al-Ghazali does find what he is looking for and in the process, reconciles orthodox faith with the mystical. It is a momentous resolution and reconciliation of two often opposing streams of religion. Ibn Arabi gives up his comfortable life in Andalusia and takes to the path of Sufi travel from which he never really returns.

I have already referred to the *ilm*-ethos. The Quran mentions *ilm* more than any other word except the name of God and the Prophet of Islam, peace be upon him, has dozens of sayings emphasizing the importance of knowledge for every Muslim man or woman, such as "the ink of the scholar is more sacred than the blood of the martyr." At its height, Muslim civilization promoted knowledge and learning.

The Muslim philosophers were inspired by the two of the greatest attributes of Allah, compassion and mercy, and the example of the Prophet of Islam, who is defined in the Quran as "a mercy unto mankind" (Surah 21: Verse 107). This emphasis on mercy and kindness created a confident geniality and spiritual buoyancy in society. Muslims have a remarkable sense of optimism which has survived into our times in spite of the severe challenges they faced and are facing in many parts of the world.

We note that the philosophers of the Golden Age provided a philosophy of purpose and meaning to life. It helped create an overarching optimism and belief that all would be well. By pursuing knowledge, learning, and compassion, society was striving towards an ideal. In contrast, the sense of purposelessness that invites cynicism and despair is the bane of modern civilization.

Often overlooked is the fact that Islam, through its *ilm*-ethos, instilled in individuals who saw learning as the path to the Divine and a method of self-improvement the urge to promote a culture of goodness. The Quran constantly asks its readers to look at the heavens, the nations and states, and consider the vast variety of human communities with their different languages, and to wonder. It instills in us the constant urge to examine and inquire. Just looking around and marveling at the world around us instills in us what would be called centuries later after the coming of Islam, the "scientific" mind or the "inquiring" mind.

Islam requires us to look at life in a holistic manner, to see its different parts as interconnected, with one thing leading to another. It emphasizes that we must have faith in our destiny and live up to the ideals of being human through scholarship, good behavior, and piety. Even inculcating these values on a basic level can remove the cynicism, depression, disillusionment, and anger that are so prevalent today.

The Flying Man

Mongols besieging Baghdad in 1258, painting circa 1430-1434 from Rashid al-Din's Jami al-tarawikh

We can learn from recent health and nutrition literature about the importance of movement. Islamic society encourages the individual to keep moving. There is the larger movement, as Muslims must proceed on various pilgrimages, including the Hajj, the pilgrimage to Mecca at least once in a lifetime. There is the travel and pursuit of better opportunities in employment and learning. There is then the constant movement during the day, as the five daily prayers require rigorous ablutions and standing, bending and prostrating in worship. Many worshipers prefer to walk for at least one of the daily prayers to the nearest mosque. Islamic daily prayers, along with the reading of the Quran, make the worshipper aware of spirituality and the dangers of being seduced by excessive materialism. God repeatedly asks you to live a contented and clean life but also warns you of the dangers of being obsessed with material possessions, with which you can never be satiated.

THE ABRAHAMIC ELEMENTS OF AN IDEAL SOCIETY

Several Islamic concepts help us on our journey. *Ihsan*, for example, is a beautiful Quranic concept that broadly translates as "beauty," "excellence," or "balance." Through the spiritual essence of *ihsan*, we understand divinity and know that its light is reflected in each one of us. Another concept is that of *ibadat* or worship. It has a two-way purpose: it is devotion to God and therefore points to the Divine and is addressed to the Divine, but it also points back at you as it comes directly from and goes back to your heart and is therefore about connecting you with what brings you peace and calm. *Ibadat* thus blesses you twice over—as you come closer to the Divine and as you find greater peace in your heart. The philosophers of the Golden Age reminded us of our purpose in life. By pursuing knowledge, learning, and compassion, they were striving towards a state of harmony and peace.

Why and how did the Golden Age of Islam come to an end? The period of history had run its course; corrupt and inaccessible rulers, increasing persecution of scholars, and indifference to the plight of the poor had begun to take their toll. The Arab world was already weakened by the repeated assaults of the Crusaders from the west when the Mongols launched their attack. The end came with the Mongol assault on Baghdad, the capital of the Abbasid dynasty, in 1258. The attack was equivalent to the atomic bombs which destroyed Hiroshima and Nagasaki. It is estimated that the Mongol army was accompanied by a quarter of a million battle-hardened horsemen. Between 200,000 and 2 million civilians were brutally slaughtered. One of the first targets was the Grand Library, where hundreds of thousands of books were thrown into the rivers, turning the water black. The Mongol armies destroyed not only books and libraries but also ancient irrigation systems, causing irreparable damage to the local economy. By slaughtering the Caliph in a very public and humiliating manner, the Mongols conveyed to the Muslim world that the head and symbol of the Abbasid empire had been crushed ignominiously.

But the Mongols were not done yet. Like a storm gathering pace, the Mongol armies moved inexorably westward, exterminating one great Muslim center of learning and power after another, including Aleppo, Damascus, and eventually Cairo. If Cairo had fallen, the way to Europe would have been open across North Africa and the Maghreb, and Europe would have been in a classic pincer movement between two Mongol forces on the eastern and western borders of the continent. However, Sultan Qutuz of Egypt had other plans. He gathered his Mamluk army and, joined by his rival Baybars, met the Mongols in a ferocious clash of armies at Ain Jalut in 1260. The battle moved back and forth almost equally between the two fierce forces until Qutuz tore off his helmet, lifted his head towards the heavens, invoked Allah, and charged at the enemy forces. The sight of their leader fearlessly throwing caution to the wind electrified the Mamluk army, and with renewed vigor, they followed Qutuz and defeated the Mongols. The Mamluks had won one of the most decisive battles in history. Just as Saladin had won a great victory over the Crusaders at Hatin and recovered Jerusalem, Qutuz and Baybars had defeated the hitherto invincible Mongol army at Ain Jalut.

The Crusaders from the west and the Mongols from the east had battered and bruised the Muslim world and brought it to its knees, but it had survived. What had been severely, perhaps fatally, damaged, however, was the idea and practice of the *ilm*-ethos. Even the most dedicated scholar ideally requires pen and paper, books and libraries, students and schools, and above all, peace of mind and security to pursue scholarship. The onslaught on the Muslim world had effectively brought to a close the Golden Age of scholarship. There were other great subsequent Muslim empires and scholars, but the Arab world had passed from history and would never again recover its preeminent position.

CONCLUSION: THE RELEVANCE OF THE PHILOSOPHERS TO OUR TIMES

Picture yourself standing alone on a deserted beach by the ocean when you see a ferocious tsunami already a hundred feet high hurtling towards you. That is precisely where we are standing as a world civilization facing the future. The list of threats is short but deadly: climate change, religious violence and genocide, the phobias attached to particular peoples, Islamophobia, anti-Semitism, and pandemics; this is not even counting the dangers of technological developments such as AI, which can out-run and out-kill homo sapiens and will soon be able to out-think

The Flying Man

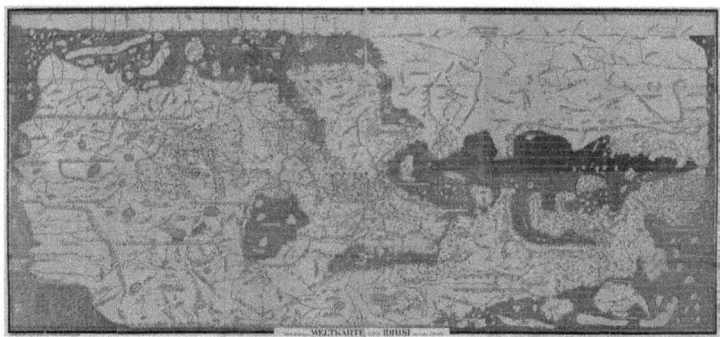

The Tabula Rogeriana, drawn by al-Idrisi for Roger II of Sicily in 1154, one of the most advanced medieval world maps.

them. Each one of these is a threat in itself, but combined they are an extinction-level event.

Standing alone on that beach, you are acutely aware that you cannot resist the danger that is coming on your own. Muslims and non-Muslims, Abrahamic and non-Abrahamic believers, atheists and humanists, everyone must mobilize their intelligence and pool their resources to meet the challenges we face. For a split second, your mind falls back to the idea of our leaders coming to our rescue and your heart sinks. You realize that rarely in history has mankind been served by a crop of leadership as poor as the one available today. Where we need wisdom, compassion, and courage, we have, with a few honorable exceptions, indifference, ignorance, and arrogance. Leaders of major nations have been energetically applauding the throwing of infants into cages after separating them from their families, and they have been systematically conducting the genocide of minorities. Leaders of today, again with some exceptions, notoriously stoke ethnic and religious passions, well aware of the dangerous and deadly game they are playing. Islamophobia, anti-Semitism, and xenophobia stalk the planet almost unchecked.

Conclusion: The Relevance of the Philosophers to Our Times

So what can the past masters we have discussed in this book teach us? There is no time to sit and study the tomes these philosophers wrote to extract lessons for our predicament, yet they have lessons for us which may just save humanity. The first step is to promote education and knowledge within our respective cultures broadly and consistently. The next step is to specifically show respect to the other and to promote what the Andalusians called "La Convivencia" or Co-Existence. We recall that the Umayyad ruler of Cordoba had a Jewish Chief Minister and a Bishop as his foreign minister, that King Roger II of Sicily would not sit on his throne until his Muslim advisor Al-Idrisi had first taken his seat. And who can forget what Frederick II, *stupor mundi*, pulled off when the Muslim world handed him Jerusalem in the middle of the Crusades without a battle due to the mutual respect and honor he had cultivated with the Muslims.

Today, neighboring nations and religions are prepared to shed blood rather than concede a single argument or an inch of land to solve a problem. The lesson is to learn to recognize our common humanity and with it our vulnerabilities. With that, the building of faith in our common humanity can begin. Simply put, the past masters remind us of the importance of having faith, of possessing the capacity to improve and change ourselves through knowledge and compassion. The past masters teach us faith, and by faith, I mean the belief in man in the broadest sense, in our common humanity, and for those who seek it, faith in a higher power. We know how Ibn Arabi was inspired by Jesus and saw him as his special guide and friend, and we read Rumi's love poems dedicated to Jesus. By these steps, the scholars are providing us the armor that will protect and preserve us and ensure our safety while promoting understanding.

They help us realize that although AI is composed of steel, wires, and computers, it cannot feel what we humans call compassion and human love. Empathy for the person you are in dialogue with is a prerequisite for a meaningful conversation. Thus, standing alone on the beach, we may feel like citizens of Baghdad in the 13th century waiting for the raging storm to hit. Nevertheless, we must not lose heart as the message of Rumi and Ibn Arabi endures, while the destroyers of cities and libraries have come and gone like the wind, leaving nothing behind.

We have identified the problem and provided a solution, and as sentient and intelligent beings, we must promote the solution. It is not rocket science. Although our philosophers have much to teach us, we must learn from their wisdom before we are stranded on the beach alone. This is the relevance of the philosophers of the Golden Age of Islam.

◊ THE DARK CLOUDS OF ISLAMOPHOBIA

While the period of European colonization is over, its deep, deleterious, and long-lasting impact is still evident. Millions of Muslims speak English or French and enjoy sports like cricket and football, but nothing can compensate for the undermining of Islamic institutions, culture, leadership, and centers, as well as the loss of confidence that may not be easily restored. The colonial era devastated the structure and values of a thousand years of indigenous scholarship, and it is hard to forget Lord Macaulay's dismissive attitude towards the entire corpus of Arabic and Sanskrit scholarship in the 19th century, declaring it not worth one bookshelf of a Western library. With his 'Minute on Education' policy directive, he consigned centuries of Arabic and Persian learning to the rubbish heap of history.

Conclusion: The Relevance of the Philosophers to Our Times

Modern civilization can be forgetful and insensitive when it comes to the past. Every new generation has a shorter memory of what has gone before them. Henry Ford famously dismissed history with his quip: "History is more or less bunk." However, there is much that we can learn from our philosophers of the Golden Age. They teach us to think logically and rationally and encourage us to invent things. Above all, they remind us that compassion and balance or *ihsan* are at the heart of our vision of life, and that knowledge itself is a form of worship. These are valuable lessons that the present generation can learn, especially when preparing for the difficult times we are living in.

Islamophobia can be defined as hatred and suspicion towards Muslims and their faith. This engenders prejudices, which often lead to violence against the community. A seminal document on this subject is *Islamophobia: A Challenge for Us All*, prepared by the Runnymede Commission in 1997, on which I had the honor of being a Commissioner. The hatred towards Muslims or Islamophobia is similar to the hostility against the Jewish community, known as anti-Semitism. There is a similar report about anti-Semitism entitled *A Very Light Sleeper*, published in 1994 by Runnymede, on which I also had the honor of serving as Commissioner. The current widespread antipathy towards Muslims and their vulnerability in many parts of the world has perpetuated what we recognize as Islamophobia. The constant stories of Muslims committing acts of terror has not helped the situation.

Year after year, I teach a popular course called the "World of Islam." Every new batch of students comes with natural optimism, but also with the damaging effects of the depiction of Islam after 9/11, in which Islam was quite deliberately distorted and the American public was misinformed. The discussion of Islam has been touched by the widespread Islamophobia to some degree. For a teacher like me, who wishes to deal in facts, it is like starting from scratch. It is always gratifying to see how these same students seem awakened by the end of term and eager to learn for themselves, feeling a slight sense of having been let down by the educational and social system in the way they were educated about Islam. After two decades of debate around Islam since 9/11, there is an awareness that if you humiliate and taunt a community, it will be resentful and angry. This applies to adults as it does to school children who will grow up hating the system that has made their lives miserable.

This topic was addressed by *South Park* in a 2019 episode titled "Mexican Joker." In the episode, Kyle is detained by ICE agents and sent to a camp on the southern border of the US. Eric Cartman, with his cruel and nasty nature, falsely reports the innocent Kyle to ICE. Kyle is not alone in the camp as there are dozens of small Mexican children with him. When the guards discover that Kyle is Jewish, they become agitated, believing that he should not be there and needs to be released immediately. Witnessing the brutal treatment of the children, Kyle warns the guards that the children's unhappiness and anger could turn one of them into a future "Mexican Joker" who symbolizes hatred against society and is out to destroy it. The guards take this to mean that there is already a Mexican Joker among the children, and a frantic effort to locate the Joker begins, the point being that the stupidity of the officials can end up creating the problem they had wished to avoid.

I believe the roots of Islamophobia lie in our teaching of history. I have always been intrigued by the concept of the so-called Dark Ages in Europe. When I looked up the time period, I was surprised to find it coincided with the Golden

Conclusion: The Relevance of the Philosophers to Our Times

Age of Islam, on the same continent. I wondered how anyone could call an age "dark" when it contained the likes of the philosophers we are discussing, both Muslim and non-Muslim. I can only conclude that this is a deliberate attempt to ignore and even misinform about what was happening in one part of the European continent. The only way to move forward is to catch up for lost time and vigorously introduce courses on the Golden Age of Islam and the accomplishments of its scientists, astronomers, mathematicians, philosophers, and poets. There is a great deal of ground to cover, and the exercise must not be delayed any longer.

I believe there is no better antidote to Islamophobia than the voices of Muslim philosophers from the Golden Age. Their calm, rational voices, rooted in logic and common sense, contrast with the hysteria of contemporary commentators. Although we tend to think of current Islamophobic writing as a new phenomenon tied to the events of 9/11, there are clear echoes from the past.

The philosophical debates among the Muslim philosophers we are discussing were often conducted in the context of an aggressive form of Christianity emerging from Europe, with the Crusades and the reconquest of Spain in mind. Christian Europeans often saw Muslims, including scholars, in a negative light. Now, with large numbers of writers and intellectuals in the United States and Europe very self-consciously "secular," the nature of the debate may have changed, but how they view Muslims and Muslim intellectuals has not. The attitude of Western intellectuals and the self-appointed champions of secularism who target Islam, such as Richard Dawkins and Sam Harris, is no longer that of a reasonable tweed-wearing uncle smoking a pipe and standing by the fireside while speaking dispassionately about abstract ideas, but is more like a mean-spirited and foul-mouthed warden in charge of the caged and terrified infants at the southern border of the US. These negative views of Muslims have global resonance and intersect with Islamophobia in different parts of the world. In India, where any calamity is blamed on the Muslim minority, leading to lynching and stabbing, even the arrival of the coronavirus was attributed to the Muslims as the "Corona jihad."

Negative perceptions of Islam start early in European history. Let me refer to an example taken from one of Europe's most celebrated literary creations, Dante's *The Divine Comedy*. In the *Comedy*, we have a major source of how Christian Europe viewed some of the foremost Muslim figures in our own study. One of Dante's ancestors, whom he wrote about in the *Comedy*, had gone to the holy lands with the Crusaders and died there. Dante was, therefore, reflecting the normative negative view of Islam. His depiction of the Holy Prophet (peace be upon him) and Hazrat Ali is grossly disrespectful and will be rejected by Muslims everywhere. Yet Dante mentions Averroes and Avicenna with a degree of honor or "onore," a word used eight times to describe them. It is well to recall that for Europeans, Averroes and Avicenna deserved credit and gratitude for salvaging the Greek philosophers like Aristotle and their intellectual tradition. Dante writes of Averroes and Avicenna as scholars of "great authority," and though he sees them as "unbelievers," they are still "virtuous." Despite Dante's generally hostile feelings towards Islam, he displays an admiration and recognition for Sultan Saladin similar to Averroes and Avicenna. This is on account of the mercy and chivalry Saladin consistently displayed after he conquered Jerusalem, including, among other things, reinstating the right of Jews to settle in Jerusalem. So, while these Muslim figures still find themselves in Dante's Hell, he captures the nuances of how they are seen by contemporary Europeans.

The equivalent of the prejudices of Dante in our times is represented by the Islamophobic polemicists who suddenly appeared in large numbers after 9/11. Although apparently well-funded, they rarely approach any level of scholarship. It was soon difficult to distinguish between the work of the polemicists and the scholars in their anxiety to write negative material about Islam. This put Muslim scholars on the defensive. From high-minded philosophy, they were now forced to consistently react to Islamophobic attacks about the nature of their religion and the danger it supposedly posed to the world. As we have seen, the philosophers of old debated the ontological and eschatological meta-issues of existence, but they were sure about their faith and its intrinsic worth. Considering the hysterical titles purporting to describe Islam, the Muslim intellectual shows remarkable sanguinity. Titles like *The Crisis of Islam*, *Christians, Muslims and Islamic Rage*, and *Radical Islam Rising* hint at material not easy to digest philosophically but make for the promise of sensationalist reading.

It is no coincidence that a spate of books targeting Muslims with a mixture of pseudoscientific arguments and thinly disguised religious prejudices came pouring out straight after 9/11 when Islamophobia was kick-started as a national phenomenon. While many authors argued that Islam itself was inherently violent, others framed their arguments in the context of religion generally and reached the conclusion that religion was violent and Islam, after 9/11, the worst culprit. Note, for example, the year of publication of Sam Harris's *The End of Faith: Religion, Terror, and the Future of Reason* (2005), Richard Dawkins's *The God Delusion* (2006), and

Christopher Hitchens's *God is not Great: How Religion Poisons Everything* (2007). All these books were produced a few years after 9/11.

From the nineteenth century onwards, philosophers with a moral conscience like Marx and Nietzsche, living in faith-based societies, moved away from religion, declaring God is dead. So, what authors like Christopher Hitchens, Richard Dawkins, and Sam Harris have been writing and saying is not new. What is new is their decidedly angry tone and focus on Muslims. It is as if Muslims were the last faithful believers in God, and they needed to be singled out, publicly humiliated, and assaulted. Every calumny and every outrage was laid on their doorstep. Where none existed, they were invented out of nothing.

The anti-Semitism that lurks under the surface has a similar source of hatred. In a fiery debate between Rabbi Shmuley Boteach and Christopher Hitchens at 92Y in New York in 2008, the rabbi turned the tables on the atheist and called him a "fundamentalist," "close-minded," and "fanatic," adjectives normally used derisively about people who believe in religion.

Even the charming and amiable Stephen Fry, himself with a Jewish mother, was not immune to an outburst against God, calling him a "maniac" and "utterly, utterly evil." "Why should I," he indignantly asked, "respect a capricious, mean-minded, stupid God who creates a world which is so full of injustice and pain?" Neither the anger nor the arguments are new. The language of the affable comedian is vulgar, meant to shock, and it does. If Fry intends to understand God, perhaps Ibn Arabi's teachings would be the best way. This is equally true for his colleagues who are similarly disenchanted. Hitchens and Fry have come out of the Oxford and Cambridge cultural matrix, where they learned to sharpen their wit even at the cost of substance. They reflect Disraeli perfectly: "A sophistical rhetorician, inebriated with the exuberance of his own verbosity." Dawkins and Harris are different. Their stolid arguments are meant to bludgeon the opposition. Wearing robes, a turban, and a flowing beard, they could pass as humorless, fire-breathing mullahs in a mosque in the Middle East. Their venomous attacks on Islam reflect the mullahs' fiery denunciations of the US and the UK as the Great Satan and the Little Satan respectively.

With his base at Oxford University as a respected professor and his high media profile, Richard Dawkins is one of the most prominent critics of religion, especially Islam. He is mocked in the *South Park* 2006 episode "Go God Go," in which Eric Cartman is frozen on a mountaintop because he cannot wait a few weeks for a new Nintendo Wii video game. Inadvertently, he is buried under an avalanche. When he is defrosted, he discovers that 500 years have passed and the planet is divided into two main groups at war with each other, both believing in different versions of atheism. Their slogan is, "science be praised."

In the episode, Professor Richard Dawkins pays a visit to the children's school. He explains the evils of religion by pointing out that Muslims were killing Jews, etc., and religion was the source of conflict in the world. Dawkins promotes atheism so successfully that eventually the entire planet becomes atheist. Later, Dawkins has feces thrown at him in class by Mrs. Garrison, a transvestite, who he later has sex with. When he discovers that his lover was in fact a man, Dawkins runs out of the house in disgust. "Have fun mocking God in hell. You faggot," shouts Mrs. Garrison.

Dawkins, who has publicly and cruelly mocked others, especially people of faith, could not bear to be mocked himself. He confessed that it was the only episode of the show he had watched, and that he was not amused. Dawkins took the matter badly, reprimanding the *South Park* team: "I'm buggered if I like being portrayed as a cartoon character buggering a bald transvestite. I wouldn't have minded so much if it had only been in the service of some serious point, but if there was a serious point in there, I couldn't discern it."[24] He added: "That isn't satire because it has nothing to do with what I stand for. And the scatological part, where they had somebody throwing shit, which stuck to my forehead—that's not even funny. I don't understand why they couldn't go straight to the atheists fighting each other, which has a certain amount of truth in it. It reminded me of the bit from Monty Python's *Life of Brian* with the Judean People's Front and the People's Front of Judea."[25]

Along with authors like Dawkins, there were dozens of less sophisticated commentators from newly established centers jumping into the fray to attack Islam. They were not serious scholars but polemicists and activists who knew that the best method to getting heard, given the climate, was to discredit Islam. This is why the twisting and distorting of facts into the present stereotypical mold of Islamophobia took place. People wanted their generally negative ideas of Islam to be confirmed, and these authors were happy to oblige. The idea was not to encourage or have a debate; it was to end it.

Their tactics resulted in spreading fear and hatred of Muslims. They were tainted because it was soon established that they were paid handsome sums to continue attacking Islam.[26] These well-oiled and well-funded centers were strategically spread throughout the US and were effective in preventing a true understanding of Islam. They made the task of inter-faith bridge-building harder. The Islamophobes spread their mephitic ideas, and their tactics succeeded in spreading a generally negative image of Islam in society. Their palingenetic argument of the need for the white race to struggle for survival against the threat of extinction from predatory forces such as Islam became one of the important strands that helped Donald Trump win the presidency in 2016. One of the first steps a grateful Trump took on entering the White House was to surround himself with some notorious Islamophobes who helped him issue the unprecedented "Muslim ban."

For the record, we should note that while the sanctimonious believer condemns the atheist or the secularist for a lack of human compassion, it is often what they see as a lack of compassion in religious followers that propels them to condemn religion. The atheist often points to religious cruelty in the past and what is happening today, giving examples of the fanatic aspects of religion as the cause of bloodshed. It is a simplistic argument but an effective one. Atheists are often motivated by concern for humanity. The assumption that the atheist is by default a cold and uncaring person is simply a stereotype. Some of the most caring individuals acting on behalf of the vulnerable, the poor, and the less privileged are self-declared atheists such as Stephen Fry and Christopher Hitchens. Correlating absence of human compassion and atheism is a weak and faulty argument not supported by empirical evidence.

In the midst of the gloom of our uninspiring record of human empathy, there are noble examples of non-Muslims who have acted with magnificent benevolence towards Muslims—Charles De Gaulle granting independence to Algeria at the risk of his life, Angela Merkel welcoming one million refugees into Germany, Jacinda Ardern expressing warm support for the Muslim community after the brutal killings at the mosques in New Zealand, and Pope Francis washing and kissing the feet of Muslim refugees in an act of Christ-like humility and love.

In the meantime, across the world, entire communities, including old men and women, children and infants, were subjected to cruel persecution during the terrible pandemic in 2020. These communities included those in Gaza, the Uighur in China, the Rohingya in Myanmar, and those in Kashmir and Yemen. But there was also widespread cruelty inflicted on communities in Syria, Iraq, and Afghanistan. It is not difficult to see why ordinary Muslims across the world were coming to the conclusion that the most persecuted people in our time were their fellow Muslims. The world, it seemed, did not care, or perhaps was too exhausted and overwhelmed to show compassion and reach out to these communities in any significant way. What these communities were experiencing was a slow inexorable form of racial and cultural genocide.

This, I thought, was happening with a full-fledged COVID-19 onslaught affecting everyone in the community while paralyzing whatever little health and educational facilities were available. Another tragedy, an invisible one this time, was unfolding: the august voices of Western liberalism, democracy, and human rights that had loudly and aggressively boasted of these values were muffled or silent in the cases of clear human rights violations involving Muslims. Human rights, they seemed to be saying, yes, for us, but not for you. It is said that large numbers of dead and dying are a statistic and do not make quite the same impact as the death of an individual.

Conclusion: The Relevance of the Philosophers to Our Times

As the pandemic devastated the world, Zeenat and I, living in lockdown in Washington DC, heard talk of war with Iran and the dangers of big power rivalry that forecast global conflict between the US and China. We saw the continued persecution of African-Americans and minorities in the US. We heard of children locked in cages on the southern borders of the US and the heartless voices of the senior-most officials of the administration justifying their cruel actions. In the midst of these depressing developments, one individual act captured the terrible zeitgeist and ethos of the age.

I saw it on live television in 2020, and the scene is forever fixed in my mind and haunts me. It is of a stout policeman forcefully pushing his knee into the neck of George Floyd, already handcuffed and lying face down pinned to the ground, and while gasping that he could not breathe, life was slowly squeezed out of him. This was on live television. No crime justified the brutal action. Floyd's transgression amounted to using a counterfeit bill of 20 dollars. The questions that bubbled up in my mind every time I thought of George Floyd were: What was the price of an African-American life in the US today? What had happened to the much-vaunted Christian concepts of mercy and justice? Considering the protests that immediately followed his death, was a sacrifice always required to awaken the conscience of the world?

On the other side, we cannot ignore the violence emerging in Muslim societies with a regularity that demands answers. It is as if the events of 9/11 acted as a catalyst, unleashing pent-up emotions and forces in Muslim societies. While we need to analyze and discuss the violence, we cannot condone or find justification for it. There are too many examples of violence, whether committed by Muslims living in the West or Muslims in societies shattered by foreign invasions in the Middle East, Afghanistan, or Africa. Explanations have not been satisfactory: the economic factor, which argues that better-off people do not commit violence; or the gender factor, which suggests that only males are involved in violence; or the argument that only those living in Muslim lands are susceptible to bloodthirsty acts do not quite explain the bloodshed.

Unfortunately, we note that the generalized bloodshed has affected both perpetrators and victims, pushing aside concepts of compassion and mercy. There is a danger of these noble concepts being replaced by shards of cynicism, fear and anger. Murder and mayhem of any kind are not acceptable and must be vigorously challenged both through the law and socially. It is a failure on the part of Muslims not to be able to find sufficiently strong answers and strategies to check and contain the ferocity. If we recognize that the bloodshed emanates from a bigger problem of a failure of vision and direction, then our philosopher-scholars have much to teach us.

I thought of the Mongols and the Crusaders, who fell on our philosophers like lightning and thunderbolts, and I thought of Ibn Arabi and Rumi, who found tranquility within themselves and were thus able to translate the cruelty and hatred around them into mystic verses that created a vision of peace and harmony. What is the answer to the hatred and anger that communities face in our time? Perhaps the first step is to learn from the masters of the past.

◊ THE WISDOM OF THE PAST MASTERS

At a time when global crises like the COVID-19 pandemic, climate change, racial strife, and religious and ethnic violence continue to rage unabated, discussions of the Flying Man and the Muslim philosophers of a bygone era may appear to some as a bit like discussing the comparative merits of the Romantic Poets and the use of iambic pentameter in Shakespeare's sonnets while sipping tea aboard the deck of the sinking Titanic, as the band nearby plays resolutely on.

If the Titanic is a metaphor, then our philosophers from the past are lifeboats ready to rescue the passengers. The spiritual dynamism and resilience of the scholars make me hopeful. Social media today makes their ideas and lives accessible on a scale as never before in history. It is a cause for celebration as now the young can begin to reclaim their spiritual and cultural legacy. No longer is the information on the scholars restricted. This development not only affects Muslims living in the West but also Muslims in Muslim lands such as Egypt, Pakistan, and Indonesia.

I am not alone in my optimism. Professor Seyyed Hossein Nasr retains an optimistic outlook concerning Islam's legacy into the next generation, seeing hopeful buds growing in Muslim society that augur well for the future. Nasr's optimism is a remarkable testimony to his own deep faith, considering he lost his priceless collection of rare manuscripts, vases, jewelry, houses, and estates when he had to leave Iran abruptly after the Iranian revolution and arrived in the West with his family to restart his life. It reminded me of so many of our philosophers from the past who faced an abrupt change of fortune and in the process lost their material wealth and precious books, including in some cases their family members. Yet their deeper faith sustained them, and their misfortune became part of their spiritual growth and creative dynamism.

We are aware that the great philosophers of the past have a direct message of hope and inspiration for us as we face the daunting challenges of our age. They embodied the beauty and grace of the human spirit. When we complain of the deadly pandemic and the religious wars around us, we ought to recall that Ibn Arabi and Rumi lived at a time during which the Muslim world faced an onslaught of hyper-aggressive attacks mounted by the Mongols from the east and the European Crusaders from the west. It is in spite of these existential threats, living in the midst of political tumult, that Ibn Arabi and Rumi were able to create and nurture their vision of love and compassion through their writings; serenity at the heart of disintegration and destruction. If nothing else, we should hold onto this thought.

Our philosophers embody the irrepressible courage of the human spirit. Despite being jailed, losing their fortunes, and sometimes their families, they never abandoned their pursuit of knowledge. They are the living incarnation of the Prophet's saying that "the ink of the scholar is more sacred than the blood of the martyr," and that the pursuit of knowledge is a form of worship. While money and power undoubtedly matter, these scholars have established the crucial importance of knowledge which overrides other activities. It is the acquisition of knowledge that not only gives wisdom but provides a means to worship. Recall Avicenna and Averroes landing in prison due to the whims of society, but still continuing their scholarly pursuits. Anticipating the inevitable clash with authority, Al-Ghazali and Ibn Arabi bade farewell to their comfortable lives and took to the Sufi path, keeping a safe distance from the corrosive influences of wealth and power.

The first lesson for us is the importance of understanding the Divine through the human heart. People are more attracted to the mystical side of each other's faiths than formal rituals or doctrines. The mystic conveys universal emotions that touch the heart, whereas formal orthodox doctrines are

Conclusion: The Relevance of the Philosophers to Our Times

seen as related to matters of the head, and their appeal is relatively restricted. This explains why Muslim figures such as Ibn Arabi and Rumi attract non-Muslims and why Christian saints like Saint Francis of Assisi are beloved by non-Christians. The appeal is the mystical dimensions that are universal to human societies.

Secondly, from them we learn the scientific and rational approach to life and religion. For the most part, they had comfortably resolved the tension between reason and revelation, between science and religion, and bridged the gap between the two. Diversity and dialectics were indispensable to scientific thought and the advancement of knowledge, but they were also important to truly understand the essential message of the Divine and the complexity of creation. Our philosophers thus brought together the streams of reason and revelation through logic and rational argument. It was one of the major contributions made by our philosophers, and one that influenced St. Thomas Aquinas directly, and therefore Christianity. Science without faith too often was stripped of the compassion that was essential to human relations, and faith without reason and logic was little more than the blind repetition of half-understood and often garbled formulae and rituals.

Today, in many parts of the world, the gap is so wide that it is common to believe that science and religion are intrinsically incompatible. The more one is of one thing, the less he/she is of the other. It is often believed in Muslim society that science, by definition, suggests the abandonment of faith. The spirit of scientific inquiry which sat comfortably with religion in the past appears to be lost and needs to be revived. Our philosophers show that you can be a philosopher, scientist, or medical physician and still be a practising and believing

Muslim. The split between reason and revelation that seems to be characteristic of society today is artificial and detracts and distorts our understanding of both science and religion.

Each and every one of the three existentialist crises that we face as a world civilization—the pandemic, the threats from climate change, and the collapsed relationships between different religions, which have led and are leading to mass violence—is attenuated by applying a combination of reason and hope that springs from the deeper wells of faith. It can only augment the human mind and, therefore, the human condition.

In the face of the reality of the Muslim world today, one question continued to raise itself again and again as I worked on this study, and I could not avoid it. How and why did the civilization which had produced such rich scholarship for half a millennium implode to its current very mediocre standard in education in the Muslim world today?

We could simply answer the question above with another experiment: We start with the three Abrahamic religions—Judaism, Christianity, and Islam—each one emphasizing the importance and pursuit of knowledge as a vital spiritual activity. The Rabbis of Judaism have acted as a store of learning and scholarship. Christianity has emphasized the "word," although the church at some stages had difficulty with its scholars. Islam has always had a healthy attitude towards knowledge, as is evident in the fact that it is the second most used word in the Quran after the name of God. For a thousand years, Islam took the lead in knowledge, and for a long time, Muslims were at the cutting edge of astronomy, mathematics, logic, metaphysics, law, and literature. Yet even a cursory glance at the situation now half a millennium later will show us how far Islam has fallen behind the other two Abrahamic faiths.

Conclusion: The Relevance of the Philosophers to Our Times

Take the Nobel prizes: Muslims have only won 12 prizes, in spite of the fact that the Muslim population is almost two billion, or about one-fourth of the global total. The religion that once produced outstanding scientists, astronomers, mathematicians, and physicians has only won three Nobel prizes for science. In contrast, the Jewish population, which is around 15 million, has won over 200 Nobel prizes. The question is why has the religion which once led the way fallen so far behind? And how did the other two do so well and still maintain the high position they have given to knowledge in their societies?

While on the subject of Nobel prizes, a discussion I had in class with a group of middle-level civil servants in Pakistan may shed light on the matter. We were participants in a course at the Rural Academy in Peshawar when a topic that is popular for discussion attracted heated comments: why Muslims do not win Nobel prizes. There were two streams of thinking. The first maintained that the West is implacably hostile to Islam and therefore Muslims are ignored and do not get prizes. The second view was that Muslims write such brilliant theses that the West cannot understand them and therefore Muslims do not win awards. I thought that while the former point of view may have some merit; the latter seemed highly improbable. The arguments were being framed in the context of colonialism and the damage it had caused, and not on a more philosophical or analytic level.

To the usual excuse, which comes easily to hand, that it was the fault of colonization, I maintain that it is not sufficiently convincing. Although I myself have reached for it instinctively, I believe the subject is worthy of greater study and investigation. If you know the secret of why Islam's sources of scholarship dried up, we can resolve them and revive Islamic scholarship. The answer lies in understanding the importance of the concept of the *ilm*-ethos. Without it, we are lost.

So, what lessons do Muslim philosophers have for us during this time of existential crisis faced by the global community? How can the knowledge and insights of the great philosophers from a thousand years ago help us with the significant global issues confronting us?

Firstly, the pandemic. It is not widely known, but as stated previously, the very notion of quarantine, social distancing, and the importance of proper hygiene in times of widespread disease came from Avicenna. In short, the measures recommended by Dr. Anthony Fauci and his colleagues to protect us from the coronavirus were already forecasted by Avicenna.

But I am referring to more than just dealing with the pandemic. Avicenna's greatest contribution was to present a philosophy of medicine that took into account physical and psychological factors, which, along with drugs and diet, created what we today call a "holistic" approach to treating the patient. When I asked Sheikh Hamza Yusuf what lessons these great sages could offer us in our time, he responded, "I think the most powerful quality the sages of our civilization consistently display, without exception, is the deep awareness that everything is from God, whether blessings or calamities. They thus acted accordingly to test people."

In asking the question of what we can learn from the Golden Age, let us again turn to the late sage Rabbi Lord Jonathan Sacks for an answer. In an interview with me in 2015, Rabbi Sacks discussed the period in European history when scholars of different faiths, like Averroes and Maimonides, read and responded to each other's work with the goal of furthering knowledge and understanding of the larger questions of existence:

Conclusion: The Relevance of the Philosophers to Our Times

> *Andalusia is one of the most important facts about our present situation. The reason is when you talk about good relations between faiths at moments of high-intensity conflict, people think you're being utopian. People just aren't that good. So, what brings these aspirations from utopia to reality is the knowledge that we have been there before. Andalusia showed how it could be done and showed that it could be done. Because of that, for me, Andalusia is the single most important feature of our current situation. We have a precedent, we know what it looked like and that's why I think the more people know about Andalusia and... there's that wonderful book by Maria Rosa Menocal called Ornament of the World, you know that's a beautiful book, but I think any study of Judaism or Christianity will see exactly how Islam contributed to these other faiths.*

Reading about our philosophers should also be a counter-argument against Islamophobia, which portrays Islam as little more than a gory religion of bloodshed, anger, and ignorance. These philosophers of old emerged from Islamic civilization and embodied it, spending their lives pursuing knowledge and contributing to the sum of human learning. I cannot help but smile wryly when I note that even a cursory reading of their work highlights one glaring point: the discussion of jihad. In its highest form, jihad has always been understood as an attempt to elevate oneself spiritually, and the lesser jihad is to defend one's family and community from violent aggression, and that too, is only to be applied within strict rules. Yet today, jihad is simply equated with murder and mayhem, which are far from Islamic teaching. If our 21st-century commentators on Islam are to be believed, jihad is at the forefront of Muslim thinking, yet it is conspicuously absent in the thought of Muslim philosophers. They were concerned with issues of the divine essence, the creation of the universe, the nature of the soul, and resurrection.

For those who harbor negative and distorted ideas of Islam, it is worth remembering these examples: Ibn Arabi saw visions of Jesus and called him his "guide" and "friend," giving away his worldly possessions and setting out on a spiritual journey in his footsteps. Averroes spent a lifetime translating Plato and Aristotle, and Avicenna and Al-Ghazali spent a great deal of time grappling with Aristotle. St. Thomas Aquinas, who has been repeatedly identified as the foremost theologian in the Roman Catholic Church by all the contemporary Popes, cited Averroes, the Muslim philosopher, 503 times in his work, and as mentioned above, so great was his reverence that he simply referred to him as The Commentator. For the record, Aquinas cited Al-Ghazali 31 times in the *Summa*. Maimonides, the greatest of the Rabbis, cited Muslim philosophers like Averroes and was given the title of Ubayd Allah, or Servant of Allah, by the appreciative Muslim society of Cairo. Jewish law and grammar were directly and deeply influenced by Islamic scholarship. And for those who believe that Muslims are anti-scientific and do not harbor a spirit of adventure, remember that the first man to attempt flight and succeed, even though it was for a few minutes, was Ibn Firnas in Cordoba. As we know, in recognition of his attempted flight, there is a bridge in the shape of huge wings in Cordoba and a crater on the moon named after him.

Avicenna teaches us the importance of experimenting with ideas in the quest to find and define the nature of God, even at the cost of upsetting orthodox scholars. Al-Ghazali teaches us to explore faith through experimentation, research, and reason. From Averroes, we learn the necessity of using logic and reason to reach conclusions, even theological ones. Ibn Arabi embodies universal humanism and compassion. Maimonides, like Averroes, uses reason and logic to approach the Jewish faith. Maimonides does for the Jewish people what Al-Ghazali, in particular, did for Muslims; creating a way of looking at the world and explaining it based on Jewish history and theology. It is an ambitious and daring project. It is precisely for this reason that his and Al-Ghazali's work remain relevant.

Al-Ghazali is currently undergoing an unprecedented revival through blogs, websites, and other digital forms. He has never been more popular as he is in the age of social media. He has also never been more misunderstood, precisely because of the superficial aspects of the age. There is a tendency among modern Muslims searching for the roots of their present predicament to categorize Al-Ghazali as a "fundamentalist": "The intellectual threat to Enlightenment Islam came from the East where the Persian theologian Al-Ghazali (d. 1111) took a literalist approach to scripture and attacked Muslim philosophers as irreligious...It was a manifesto for closing the Muslim mind, the divorce of faith and reason," wrote Ed Husain.[27] Contrary to Ed's assertion, though he is impressively moving in reconciling the various strands of his experiences with Islam, Al-Ghazali is not a threat to enlightenment; he *is* the enlightenment. He is not divorcing faith and reason; he is conducting their marriage.

Some leading Indian Muslims organized as "the Indian Muslims for Secular Democracy" were involved in a debate about the nature of Islam in 2020 and the need to condemn "Islamist" violence such as the recent gruesome beheading of a teacher in Paris, which once again precipitated a crisis across the Muslim community in Europe. So far, so good; those who murder and maim must be unequivocally condemned and severely dealt with. But what I found strange was their logic in blaming Al-Ghazali,[28] a twelfth-century scholar, for a twenty-first-century event.

In Orientalist mythology, Al-Ghazali is portrayed as a dour, bigoted Islamic mullah who rejected non-Islamic influences. In fact, by reconciling Greek philosophy and Islamic theology on the one hand and mainstream orthodox Islam and Sufi mysticism on the other, he unraveled and reconciled the issues that had plagued society. That Al-Ghazali is accused by modern writers of halting progress towards rational and progressive thinking in Islam is unfair. While he criticized Avicenna, he made it a point to praise Aristotle and his use of logic. By the end of his life, Al-Ghazali had come to be acknowledged as a *mujadid*, a reviver of faith in Islam and a saint who attracted a large number of followers.

Al-Ghazali is famous for moving formal orthodox Islam towards accepting and incorporating Sufism into the mainstream, that is, towards more personal, more direct, and more informal approaches to the divine. This was as radical as it can get. To miss out on this aspect of his teaching is sloppy scholarship. In fact, Al-Ghazali is the opposite of a fundamentalist if we use the term in the way his critics have used it; he is arguing for inclusion and acceptance. Recall that ISIS in the Middle East and the different iterations of the Taliban in Afghanistan and Pakistan have viciously and consistently targeted Sufi centers and shrines, often destroying some that are centuries old and killing hundreds in the process. Al-Ghazali's genius was to reconcile the conflicting parts of Islam in order to avoid precisely this confrontation.

Al-Ghazali was doing what Maimonides was doing for and within Judaism, and St. Thomas Aquinas was doing for

Christianity. These scholars were known and respected because they worked to enlighten and educate their communities. To impose terms such as fundamentalist or extremist, that we have created or invented in and for our times to explain social movements, onto scholars who lived a thousand years ago not only distorts their scholarship but also prevents us from comprehending the past. To call Al-Ghazali, Maimonides, or Aquinas a fundamentalist is, at best, a harmless but meaningless exercise and, at worst, a misuse of a term loaded with dangerous and ominous intent.

Averroes was received with favor in the West among non-Muslims. A philosopher who embraced knowledge, irrespective of where it came from, and based his main arguments on Plato and Aristotle was bound to be accepted favorably by Europeans. In contrast, Al-Ghazali saw himself and was seen by others as a defender and champion of Islam. He would naturally be seen in a less-than-favorable light in Europe. In time, that antipathy to Al-Ghazali filtered into the thinking of Western-trained Muslim intellectuals. Averroes was seen as "reasonable" and "progressive," what today is called a "moderate" Muslim, and Al-Ghazali as a narrow-minded "fundamentalist," terms we use today for a close-minded bigot.

So, while Averroes' contribution to philosophy was colored by Greek philosophers, what Al-Ghazali offered a complete point-by-point guide on how to live as a good Muslim in the tradition of the Prophet of Islam. None of the other philosophers, even those that were pious and exemplary Muslims, can quite match Al-Ghazali in this regard. That is not to decry or diminish the quality of their work but to point out that it is in another direction and contains different material. But Al-Ghazali is not a mere close-minded, joyless dogmatist.

Al-Ghazali makes us aware that each living creature, however big or small, has its own destiny and place in the universe. The sting of the tiny mosquito's stylets, as the Quran tells us, is as significant in the context of its size and capabilities as the power of the elephant's trunk. The purpose is for human beings to be aware of God's goodness and greatness and to remind them of the need for compassion towards all living creatures.

Al-Ghazali tells us that, from the moment we are born, we are standing before the gates of death. Therefore, we must never be heedless of our life on earth and what is to come in the future. Above all, we must be guided by the great principle laid down by the Prophet of Islam himself: the best answer to *jahiliyya*, or ignorance, is *sakina*, or peace. Compassion and forgiveness, the Prophet had said, must override everything else. That is why the Quran called him "a mercy unto mankind."

The Prophet, peace be upon him, was abused, threatened, and plans were made to assassinate him in Mecca. But there was an incident aimed at harming him that shocked even the unruly, tribal society. Hind led a campaign against the Prophet and hired the assassin Wahshi to kill Hamza, his favorite uncle. They saw their opportunity during a battle. Wahshi located Hamza and with exquisite cruelty, killed him. Hind then cut out Hamza's liver and chewed on it as a sign of contempt, a particularly insulting act in that culture. When he heard about the manner of his uncle's death, the Prophet was deeply distressed. Later, when he returned to Mecca at the head of a large army, people wondered how he would treat the two who had tormented and killed his uncle. The Prophet asked to see them to know the last minutes of his favorite uncle's life. However, when Wahshi began to describe how he jabbed and sliced Hamza, he could not hold back his tears and said, "Please stop." Now people waited for the Prophet's response. What happened next amazed the people of Mecca. The Prophet forgave the culprits and let them go free. Both were so moved and grateful that they declared they had accepted Islam. His reaction was greater than the stoic acceptance of the Greek philosophers; rather, it was an active expression of the philosophy of compassion and forgiveness as a guide to behavior.

Ibn Arabi is the champion of Sufism. In our world dominated by ideas of materialism and consumerism, the countervailing lessons of the Sufis could not be more relevant. Because Sufism deliberately exists beneath the radar, its followers are far more numerous than assumed. Like Al-Ghazali, Ibn Arabi is alive and well in the age of social media. He plays a prominent role, for example, in the internationally popular Turkish TV series on the life of Ertugrul Ghazi, the founder of the Ottoman Dynasty. Thousands of fans have been debating online whether or not Ibn Arabi looks smarter with a trimmed or full beard in the TV series. The transition from a spiritual master of a thousand years ago clouded in the mists of legend to a contemporary cultural icon is a tribute to Ibn Arabi's charisma and staying power.

Ibn Arabi's life and writings challenge many stereotypes about Islam in our age: while acknowledging the great Abrahamic prophets, he singled out Jesus as his first teacher, friend, and guide. One of his important teachers was Fatima, the female Sufi of Seville, who tells Ibn Arabi that she is his spiritual mother. His mystical writings and utterances still leave us unsure as to their exact meaning and searching for answers. The famous meeting between Averroes and Ibn Arabi is an example. Ibn Arabi considers all religions and their expressions of belief as legitimate. These religions include the Abrahamic ones like the followers of Jesus or non-Abrahamic ones like the believers in Dao. "Beware of confining yourself to a particular belief and denying all else," warns Ibn Arabi, "for much good would elude you—indeed, the knowledge of reality would elude you. Be in yourself a matter for all forms of belief, for God is too vast and tremendous to be restricted to one belief rather than another."[29] Ibn Arabi's sentiments confirm our findings in the thought experiment we conducted earlier, in which we saw the remarkable similarity in thought among the three religious heavyweights, one from each Abrahamic religion.[30]

What does the celebrated love and compassion of the Sufis mean in real and practical terms? It is the attention, the inclusion, the accessibility, the hope, and the dignity and honor they bestow on members of their circle. The individual within the Sufi orbit feels he or she belongs. It provides a strong sense of security in an uncertain world. Most importantly, the individual knows that in the Sufi master there is a strong, visible, and present figure they can turn to for advice and guidance even in trying times.

Ibn Arabi's philosophy of life and appreciation of religious pluralism are contained in these famous verses which could be an inspiration and motto for twenty-first-century society, especially for the young, as we seek ways for different communities to be able to live together in harmony and dignity:[31]

> *My heart has become capable of every form: it is a pasture for gazelles and a convent for Christian monks, and a temple for idols and the pilgrim's Kaaba and the tables of the Torah and the book of the Qur'an. I follow the religion of Love: whatever way Love's camels take, that is my religion and my faith.*

Conclusion: The Relevance of the Philosophers to Our Times

Maimonides too has a key role to play for the present generation. For most Muslims, Judaism remains forbidden territory because they equate it with Israel and its policies towards the Palestinians. Muslims and Jews therefore see each other through a mutually hostile lens. This is one of the great tragedies of the two Abrahamic faiths because of their inherent spiritual and theological proximity. Muslims reading Maimonides would appreciate how close Judaism is to Islam, and Jews also reading Maimonides would appreciate that the vision and work of the great Jewish philosopher is in consonance with the great Muslim thinkers of his age. Maimonides provides a bridge between the two religions that can become a permanent and strong link.

From Maimonides, we learn that Judaism, like Islam, preaches kindness and compassion to the other. The instructions are clear: "Any non-Jew who lives in your land needs to be treated with respect and with kindness... You should give them food and kindness. We should visit their sick and bury their dead and sustain their poor." Maimonides even praises Muslims and Christians for promoting the worship of "our Creator." In this, Maimonides identifies the children of Ismail, that is, the Prophet of Islam and the Muslim community. According to Maimonides, there is even a place in the world to come for the righteous other.

As for the relevance of Maimonides today, I saw evidence of this in a debate conducted in New York in 2016. Self-declared atheists Christopher Hitchens and Sam Harris were in debate with two prominent rabbis on the subject of Atheism and Religion. What I found interesting was that when the debate got going, both rabbis cited Maimonides, especially on the difficult theological issues such as resurrection.

St. Thomas Aquinas too is a towering figure of faith and a connecting point between religions. Non-Christians can take so much from him: the introduction to Jesus, the central figure of Christianity and to the larger Abrahamic faiths, the devotion to God, the commitment to compassion and the promotion of knowledge irrespective of its origins and the importance of reason in finding faith. St. Thomas Aquinas embodies the great Christian virtues of piety, humility, forgiveness, austerity, charity, and the commandment to love one another. He was a philosopher-saint for all time.

Reading the lives of these great philosophers of the Golden Age, even in a cursory fashion, should inspire Muslims and non-Muslims alike. Studying the great Muslim scholars of the past will encourage young Muslim minds to engage with serious and universal issues of life and lead them away from thoughts of conflict and revenge. They will be more focused on making sense of eternal issues such as the true purpose of life, the nature of the universe, and the question of what lies ahead for each one of us after death. They will understand that sorrow and joy are both part of life. Perhaps this will ensure that the angry young man will become the thoughtful young man.

Today, in the settlements of the Sahel, in the villages of the Punjab in Pakistan, and in the suburbs of Chicago and Los Angeles, if Muslim families are inspired by any of our philosophers, it would be by Al-Ghazali more than Avicenna or Averroes. Some young Muslims wishing to explore mysticism may want to read Rumi, who is popular in the West, and Ibn Arabi. Muslims today generally want to learn mainstream orthodox Islam rather than explore the spiritual effervescence that defined the work of the Muslim philosophers of the Golden Age. It is an Islam that is on the defensive and needs to first set its house in order. There are too many dark and dangerous threats, too many assaults all around. It is a time to circle the wagons. Al-Ghazali helps to set standards and define clearly the boundaries and parameters of the faith with the robust confidence of representing a civilization at its zenith.

As a student of history and religion, I am impressed by the scope and scale of the Muslim intellectuals of the past and cannot conceal my disappointment at the performance of their counterparts in our time, with a few honorable exceptions. The Muslim scholar of today is often met with suspicion and hostility towards their work, a lack of support, and rampant violence in their own society. Today, Muslim philosophers live dangerously close to being accused of blasphemy. Muslim leaders such as Asad in Syria, Saddam in the recent past in Iraq, or the Taliban in Afghanistan usually target scholars as being disloyal if they do not acknowledge them. The American military and its drones often wrongly target them also.

As Professor Abdul Hamid Abu Sulayman, a leading Arab scholar formerly living in the United States, explained when I asked him about the mediocrity of Muslim scholarship, "the Muslim scholar is either caught between the ignorant mullahs threatening him with *jahannum* (hell) or the corrupt rulers threatening him with jail."[32] It explains why the image that comes to mind when thinking of the Muslim scholar is not that of the Flying Man, but that of the Crying Man as he is pushed into the Nile or the Tigris-Euphrates to open-mouthed crocodiles. It explains why the image that comes to mind when thinking of the Muslim scholar is not philosophic points such as those made by the Flying Man, but the very real dangers of that of the Sinking Man.

Nonetheless, rulers and leaders of the Muslim world should read our philosophers of the past and take instruction: they should promote knowledge and learning through universities and colleges; they should patronize scholars and embrace scholarship. Ordinary people should value the wisdom and guidance of great scholars and philosophers to give them better instruction and direction in their lives. Students should be inspired by the rich legacy they have inherited and attempt to follow in the path of the philosophers. It will balance the over-emphasis on economics and IT, which creates a materialistic, economics-dominated worldview.

Through the centuries of colonization and the struggles of the local peoples to obtain independence, through the fragmentation of traditional structures and the chaos that followed, what still remains, perhaps not in full but in good measure, is the inspiring core message of the scholars and saints from the past. That is the legacy of humanity gifted by the extraordinary gathering of the scholars of the Golden Age.

Heeding them, we will be stronger and more confident to face the future. A change in the current paradigm will mean that Muslims will rediscover their own rich legacy and read about Jewish and Christian philosophers interacting with it. Jews and Christians will be introduced to Muslim philosophers. They will begin to understand how close those who use the method of rationality, logic, and reason in appreciating their destiny are to each other. The exercise will be a masterclass in genuine interfaith understanding. That, in itself, justifies the revival of the masters of the past.

Endnotes

1   This is also the subject of my new study with Frankie Martin and Dr. Amineh Hoti for the Brookings Institution Press.

2   For a discussion of the *ilm*-ethos and how it shapes society, see my *Journey into Europe*, 2018.

3   *Reason and Revelation in the Middle Ages*, 1938, p. 38.

4   See his *The Polymath: Unlocking the Power of Human Versatility*, 2019

5   E.G. Browne, *Islamic Medicine*, 2002, pp. 60–61

6   "Avicenna," *In Our Time*, with Melvyn Bragg, BBC Radio 4. 8 November 2007

7   In Dr. A. Zahoor and Dr. Z. Haq, *Quotations from Famous Historians of Science*, 1997

8   Nasr, 2007

9   Griffel, "Al-Ghazali," 2020.

10   "Al-Ghazali," *In Our Time*, with Melvyn Bragg, BBC Radio 4, 19 March, 2015

11   "Matters of Faith: Dr. Timothy Winter. The Life and Works of Al-Ghazali," hosted by Kristiane Backer, YouTube

12   *Reason and Revelation in the Middle Ages*, p. 40.

13   Anadolu Agency, 2018.

14   *Humanities*, Vol. 32, No. 6, November/December 2011

15 Fisher and Bailey, 2000, p.79

16 Ibid. p. 279.

17 For a contemporary introduction to Sufism—through the Sufi method of using stories, analogies, allegories, literary and Quranic sayings and wisdom from the sages—by a prominent Sufi master, see *Witnessing Perfection: a Sufi Guide* by Shaykh Fadhlalla Haeri, 2016, and *Spiritual Encounters: Sharing the Wisdom of the Enlightened Sufis* by Shaykh Fadhlalla Haeri and Muneera Haeri, 2018; and for the perspective of an English Sufi, see Peter Sanders' *Meetings with Mountains: Encounters with the Saints and Sages of the Islamic World*, 2019. For a classic European journey to the east in search of mysticism, see Hermann Hesse, 2011. Two other excellent books on Sufism are recommended: *Creativity: Ibn Arabi's Traditional Islamic Philosophy of Education* by Dr. Ayesha Leghari, 2017, and *Gems and Jewels* by Dr. Amineh Hoti, a study based in fieldwork in rural Pakistan, 2021.

18 "Quotes," University of California, Berkeley

19 Nissen Mangel, "Talmudist," Brooklyn, NY: Kehot Publication Society, 1985

20 Bammate, 1982, pp. 36–37

21 Pope John Paul II, *Fides et Ratio*, 1998

22 Benedict XVI, General Audience, Saint Peter's Square, 2 June 2010.

23 "Amoris Laetitia based on 'classical doctrine of Aquinas', Pope Francis says," *Catholic Herald*, 21 August 2018

24 Sean Nicholls and Leesha McKenny. "Scientist parks trannie sex jibe," *The Sydney Morning Herald*, March 4, 2010.

25 Chip Rowe, "Playboy Interview: Richard Dawkins," *Playboy*, August 20, 2012.

26 See *Fear, Inc. The Roots of the Islamophobia Network in America, Center for American Progress*, by Wajahat Ali, Eli Clifton, Matthew Duss, Lee Fang, Scott Keyes, and Faiz Shakir, August 26, 2011.

27 "Islam's Enlightenment: Muslim thinkers offer a remedy to fundamentalism," *The Spectator*, 14 November 2020.

28 *National Herald*, 26 October 2020.

29   Jorg Luyken, 2008

30   For further commentary on Ibn Arabi, see *The Garden of Truth: The Vision and Promise of Sufism, Islam's Mystical Tradition* by Seyyed Hossein Nasr.

31   From *Islamic Mystical Poetry* by Mahmood Jamal, 2009.

32   Akbar Ahmed, 2003, pp. 91-92.

Bibliography

Akbar S. Ahmed, *Islam Under Siege: Living Dangerously in a Post-Honor World* (Cambridge: Polity, 2003).

Al-Ghazali, *The Incoherence of the Philosophers*. Translated by Michael E. Marmura. (Provo: Brigham Young University Press, 2000).

Al-Ghazali, Imam Abu Hamed, *Revival of Religion's Sciences: Ihya' Ulum Al-Din*, Vol. I-IV. Translated by Mohammad Mahdi al-Sharif. (Beirut: DKI, 2011).

Al-Ghazali, *Deliverance from Error*, (al-Munqidh min al-dalal). Translated by Richard J. McCarthy (Boston: Twayne, 1980).

Anadolu Agency, "Ibn Rushd: The scholar who Forged the Knowledge of East in West," *Daily Sabah*, December 17, 2018.

Averroes, *Tahafut al-Tahafut* (The Incoherence of the Incoherence). Translated by Simon Van den Bergh. (Cambridge: Gibb Memorial Trust, 2008).

Avicenna, *The Metaphysics of The Healing*. Translated by Michael E. Marmura. (Provo, UT: Brigham Young University Press, 2005).

Binyamin Abrahamov, Ibn al-'Arabī's *Fusus Al-Hikam: An Annotated Translation of 'The Bezels of Wisdom'* (Abingdon: Oxon: Routledge, 2015).

Dante Alighieri, *The Divine Comedy*. Translated by John Ciardi. (New York: W. W. Norton and Company, 1977).

Edward C. Sachau, *Alberuni's India*, Vol. I and II. (London: Routledge, 2000).

Étienne Gilson, *Reason and Revelation in the Middle Ages* (New York: Charles Scribner's Sons, 1938).

Frank Griffel, "Al-Ghazali," *The Stanford Encyclopedia of Philosophy* (Summer 2020 Edition), Edited by Edward N. Zalta. https://plato.stanford.edu/archives/sum2020/entries/al-ghazali/.

Haidar Bammate, *Muslim Contribution to Civilization* (Takoma Park, MD: American Trust Publications, 1982).

Henry James Jacques Winter. *Eastern Science; An Outline of Its Scope and Contribution*, 1st edition (London: John Murray, 1952).

Hermann Hesse, *The Journey to the East* (Martino Publishing, CT. USA, 2011).

Jorg Luyken, "Mystical Transcendence: Is Sufism the Pluralistic Accepting Face of Islam?" (*The Jerusalem Post*, May 22, 2008).

Lenn E. Goodman, *Avicenna* (London: Routledge, 1992).

Mahmood Jamal, *Islamic Mystical Poetry: Sufi Verse from the early Mystics to Rumi* (Penguin Classics, 2009).

Mary Pat Fisher and Lee W. Bailey, eds. *An Anthology of Living Religions* (Upper Saddle River, NJ: Prentice Hall, 2000).

Michael Brenner, *A Short History of the Jews* (Princeton University Press, 2010).

Moses Maimonides, *The Guide for the Perplexed, Vol. I and II*. Translated by Shlomo Pines. (Chicago: University of Chicago Press, 1963).

Richard Joseph McCarthy, *Freedom and Fulfillment: An Annotated Translation of Al-Ghazali's Al-Munqidh Min Al-Dalal and Other Relevant Works of Al-Ghazali* (Boston: Twane, 1980).

Richard Walzer, *Al-Farabi On the Perfect State: Abu Nasr al-Farabi's Mabadi'ara' ahl al-Madina al-Fadila* (Oxford: Clarendon Press, 1985).

Seyyed Hossein Nasr, *Islam and the Plight of Modern Man* (London: Longman, 1975).

Seyyed Hossein Nasr, *The Garden of Truth: The Vision and Promise of Sufism*, Islam's Mystical Tradition (New York: HarperOne, 2007).

Thomas Aquinas, *Summa Theologica*. Translated by the Fathers of the English Dominican Province (Claremont, CA: Coyote Canyon Press, 2018).

www.ingramcontent.com/pod-product-compliance
Lightning Source LLC
LaVergne TN
LVHW011423080426
835512LV00005B/232